Skiing
and the
Art of Carving

Ellen Post Foster

Photography by Alan Schönberger

Skiing and the Art of Carving

by Ellen Post Foster

Published by the Turning Point Ski Foundation

Published by:
TURNING POINT SKI FOUNDATION
P.O. Box 246
South Hero, VT 05486 U.S.A.

Copyright © 1996 by Turning Point Ski Foundation
First Edition, 1996; Second printing, 1998
Printed in the United States of America by:
RR Donnelley & Sons Company
Harrisonburg, Virginia.

Library of Congress Catalog Card Number: 96-61455
ISBN 0-9647390-3-8 $17.95

Edited by Daniel Post, Emily Anhalt and Annette E. Gras
Photography by Alan Schönberger, except for the following:
    Dobber Price, page 221
    Ellen Post Foster, figures 1.5–1.7, 1.9–1.11, 8.3, 8.6, 8.7
Black and white drawings by Alan Schönberger, except for the following:
    Daniel Post, figure 1.8
    Peter G. Ifju, figure 1.13

Books and video available from:
Turning Point Ski Foundation
P.O. Box 943,
Edwards, CO 81632 U.S.A.
E-mail: skibooks@tpsf.org
http://www.tpsf.org/

SYNOPSIS

INTRODUCTION
LESSON PLANNING

CHAPTER 1   **A CURVED PATH**
CHAPTER 2   **DEVELOPING BALANCE**
CHAPTER 3   **TURNING IN A WEDGE**
CHAPTER 4   **PARALLEL TURNS**
CHAPTER 5   **DYNAMIC SKIING**
CHAPTER 6   **QUICK TURNS**
CHAPTER 7   **STEP TURNS**
CHAPTER 8   **DEEP SIDECUT CARVE**
CHAPTER 9   **ON THE SNOW WARM-UP**
CHAPTER 10   **PERCEPTUAL SKILLS**

GLOSSARY
APPENDIX I   **CORRECTING ERRORS**
APPENDIX II   **EQUIPMENT**
APPENDIX III   **SKI PATTERN**
APPENDIX IV   **LESSON PLAN WORKSHEET**
INDEX

DEMONSTRATORS:
  Jay Evans
  Ellen Post Foster
  Steve Olwin
  Tony Russo
  Alan Schönberger

23   **AUTHOR'S NOTES**

27   **FOREWORD** by Mike Porter

29   **INTRODUCTION**

35   **LESSON PLANNING**

CHAPTER 1

43   **A CURVED PATH**

45   **SKI DESIGN**

46   **BEND THE SKI**

47   **TIP THE SKI**

47   **A CARVED TURN**

48   **MODEL THE SKI**

48   **TERMINOLOGY**

49   **A STEERED TURN**

49   **NEW TECHNOLOGY**

CHAPTER 2

51   **DEVELOPING BALANCE**

52   **BALANCED STANCE**

52   **BODY POSITION**

53   **PRACTICE THE STANCE**

53   **BALANCE POINT**

54   *NOTES FOR DEEP SIDECUT SKIS*

54   **COMMON MISTAKES**

55   **FIRST MOVEMENTS**

55   **WALKING**

55   **GETTING UP FROM A FALL**

56   **SLIDING STEPS**

CONTENTS

CONTENTS

57   LIFT A SKI

57   SIDESTEP

57   WALK AROUND OBJECTS

58   STEP OVER OBJECTS

58   ONE SKI SCOOTER

60   **BALANCING EXERCISES**

60   SLIDE DOWNHILL

60   BALANCE ROUTINE

61   STEP OVER POLES

61   **CONTROL OF SPEED**

61   WEDGE POSITION

61   JUMP TO A WEDGE POSITION

62   SLIDE IN A WEDGE

63   VARY WEDGE WIDTH

63   WEDGE TO A STOP

64   PARALLEL AND WEDGE POSITIONS

65   **LESSON PLAN**

65   WARM YOUR BODY

66   RHYTHM AND REVIEW

66   DIRECTED FREE SKIING

66   SCHOOLWORK

67   MOUNTAIN PLAYGROUND

67   SLOW AND EASY

67   **LESSON PLAN EXAMPLE**

CHAPTER 3

69 **TURNING IN A WEDGE**

70 **TURN DESCRIPTION**
70 *NOTES FOR DEEP SIDECUT SKIS*

72 **SKILL DEVELOPMENT**

72 **WEDGE/PARALLEL**
72 **UPPER BODY POSITION**
72 **THE OUTSIDE SKI**
73 **FLEX AND EXTEND**
74 *NOTE FOR DEEP SIDECUT SKIS*
74 **THE INSIDE SKI**
75 **CARVING**
77 *NOTE FOR DEEP SIDECUT SKIS*
77 **EDGE LOCKS**
77 *NOTE FOR DEEP SIDECUT SKIS*
77 **VARY WEDGE WIDTH**
77 **UPPER BODY EXERCISE**

78 **SKI POLE ACTION**

78 **POLE STRAPS**
78 **ARM POSITION**
78 **POLING ACROSS FLAT TERRAIN**

80 **TURN SHAPE**

80 **DRAWING TURNS**
80 **HAND TURNS**
80 **STUDY ARCS**
80 **VARY TURN SIZE**
80 **CONTROL SPEED**
81 **LEAD-FOLLOW**

82 **TERRAIN AND SNOW CONDITIONS**

82 **GENTLE TERRAIN**

CONTENTS

82   **STEEPER TERRAIN**

82   **VARIABLE TERRAIN**

83   **HARD SNOW AND ICE**

83   **POWDER SNOW**

84   **CRUD SNOW**

84   **LESSON PLAN**

84   **WARM YOUR BODY**

84   **RHYTHM AND REVIEW**

84   **DIRECTED FREE SKIING**

85   **SCHOOLWORK**

85   **MOUNTAIN PLAYGROUND**

85   **SLOW AND EASY**

85   **LESSON PLAN EXAMPLE**

CHAPTER 4

87   **PARALLEL TURNS**

88   **TURN DESCRIPTION**

89   **BALANCING EXERCISES**

89   **BALANCE ROUTINE ON ONE SKI**

90   **SIDE STEP OVER POLE**

91   **SKILL DEVELOPMENT**

91   **SIDE STEP SHADOW CHASE**

91   **TRAVERSE**

91   **TRAVERSE EXERCISES**

92   **TRAVERSE TARGET**

92   *NOTE FOR DEEP SIDECUT SKIS*

92   **SIDESLIP**

94   **FORWARD SIDESLIP**

94   **BOOT TURNS**

94   **PIVOT SLIP**

95   **SAFETY STOP**

96   **GARLAND TURNS**

97   **LIFT THE INSIDE SKI**

97   **CRAYON MARK**

97   **LEAPING**

98   **BOBBING**

99   **SKATING**

100   **SKI POLE ACTION**

100   **POLE SWING**

100   **TOUCH/PLANT**

100   **TIMING OF THE POLE ACTION**

100   **INCORRECT ARM MOVEMENTS**

101   **TURN SHAPE**

101   **FOOT ARCS**

102   **SKIDDING/CARVING**

102   **VARY SIZE**

102   **CONTROL SPEED**

102   **TERRAIN AND SNOW CONDITIONS**

102   **EASIEST TERRAIN**

103   **MORE DIFFICULT TERRAIN**

103   **SMALL BUMPS**

104   **LONG TURNS IN BUMPS**

104   **TERRAIN GARDEN**

105   **TERRAIN FEATURES**

105   **HARD SNOW AND ICE**

106   **DEEP SNOW**

106   **LESSON PLAN**

106   **WARM YOUR BODY**

106   **RHYTHM AND REVIEW**

107   **DIRECTED FREE SKIING**

107   **SCHOOLWORK**

CONTENTS

108   **MOUNTAIN PLAYGROUND**

108   **SLOW AND EASY**

108   **LESSON PLAN EXAMPLE**

CHAPTER 5

109   # DYNAMIC SKIING

110   **TURN DESCRIPTION**

111   **BALANCING EXERCISES**

111   **LIFT A SKI**

112   **ROYAL**

112   **SKI ON ONE SKI**

112   **NO POLES**

113   **SKILL DEVELOPMENT**

113   **FORE/AFT BALANCE**

113   *NOTE FOR DEEP SIDECUT SKIS*

113   **ANGULATED POSITION**

114   **WEDGE/PARALLEL**

115   **BANKING**

116   **COUNTERED POSITION**

116   **ADVANCED TRAVERSE EXERCISES**

117   **JAVELIN TURNS**

118   **UPPER BODY DIRECTION**

119   **FLOATERS**

120   *NOTE FOR DEEP SIDECUT SKIS*

120   **FLOW**

120   **SPEED**

121   **SMOOTH PATH**

122   **SKI POLE ACTION**

122   **POLE ACTION**

122   *NOTE FOR DEEP SIDECUT SKIS*

122   **INCORRECT POLE ACTION**

122   **TURN SHAPE**

122   **DIFFERENT TURN SHAPES**
123   **CONSISTENT RADIUS**
123   **VARYING TURNS**

124   **TERRAIN AND SNOW CONDITIONS**

124   **GENTLE TERRAIN**
124   **MORE DIFFICULT TERRAIN**
124   **MOST DIFFICULT TERRAIN**
125   **ADVENTURE**
126   **BUMP SKIING**

126   **LESSON PLAN**

126   **WARM YOUR BODY**
126   **RHYTHM AND REVIEW**
126   **DIRECTED FREE SKIING**
126   **SCHOOLWORK**
127   **MOUNTAIN PLAYGROUND**
127   **SLOW AND EASY**

127   **LESSON PLAN EXAMPLE**

CHAPTER 6
129   **QUICK TURNS**

130   **TURN DESCRIPTION**
130   *NOTE FOR DEEP SIDECUT SKIS*

130   **BALANCING EXERCISES**

130   **SKI WITHOUT POLES**
131   **SKI "WITHOUT" BINDINGS**
132   **SKI ON ONE SKI**

132   **ONE SKI AND ONE POLE**

134   **ONE SKI AND NO POLES**

134   **SKILL DEVELOPMENT**

134   **TARGET SKIING**

134   **MOVING TARGET**

135   **MOVEMENT DOWN THE HILL**

136   **ARMS CROSSED**

136   **TUCK TURNS**

137   **HORIZONTAL POLE**

137   **HOLD HANDS**

138   **HOP TURNS**

140   **HOP TURN ENTRY**

140   **HOP TURNS ON THE OUTSIDE SKI**

142   **HOP TURN ENTRY, OUTSIDE SKI**

142   **CHARLESTON**

143   **REBOUND**

143   **SHORT TURNS ON A DIAGONAL**

143   **FORMATION SKIING**

143   **(a) Synchronized Turns**

144   **(b) Opposite Turns**

145   **(c) Lead-Follow**

145   **(d) Synchronized Speed Play**

146   **(e) Synchronized Circle**

146   **(f) Line Pull-out**

146   **(g) Long and Short Medley**

148   **SKI POLE ACTION**

148   **VERBAL CUE**

148   **POLE TIP FORWARD**

148   **ARM POSITION**

150   **POLE TIMING**

150   **DOUBLE POLE PLANT**

151   **ERROR RECOGNITION AND CORRECTION**

152   **TURN SHAPE**

151   **VARY TURNS**

152   **SMOOTH TRANSITIONS**

152   **RHYTHM CHANGES**

152   **LEAD-FOLLOW**

152   **TERRAIN AND SNOW CONDITIONS**

152   **ADAPT TO TERRAIN**

152   **VERSATILITY**

152   **STEEP TERRAIN**

154   **DEEP SNOW**

155   **CRUD SNOW**

155   **BUMP SKIING**

155   **LINE IN THE BUMPS**

157   **DIFFERENT PATHS**

158   **ADJUST DIRECTION**

158   **LESSON PLAN**

158   **WARM YOUR BODY**

158   **RHYTHM AND REVIEW**

158   **DIRECTED FREE SKIING**

158   **SCHOOLWORK**

159   **MOUNTAIN PLAYGROUND**

159   **SLOW AND EASY**

159   **LESSON PLAN EXAMPLE**

CHAPTER 7

161   **STEP TURNS**

162   **PARALLEL STEP TURNS**

162   **TURN DESCRIPTION**

164   **BALANCING EXERCISES**

164   **SIDE STEP OVER POLE**

164   **STEP DRILLS**

164   **SKILL DEVELOPMENT**

164   **STEP IN A TRAVERSE**
164   **PARALLEL STEP**
165   **PARALLEL STEP GARLAND**
167   **TRAVERSE, STEP AND TURN**
167   **STEP AND TURN**
168   **REVIEW**
168   **VARY RADIUS**

169   **CONVERGING STEP TURNS**

169   **TURN DESCRIPTION**

170   **BALANCING EXERCISES**

170   **CONVERGING STEPS IN A CIRCLE**
171   **WAGON WHEEL**
171   **ZIG-ZAG DRILL**

172   **SKILL DEVELOPMENT**

172   **CONVERGING STEP**
172   **CONVERGING STEP GARLAND**
173   **TRAVERSE, STEM AND TURN**
173   **STEM AND TURN**
174   **FALL LINE CONVERGING TURNS**

175   **DIVERGING STEP TURNS**

175   **TURN DESCRIPTION**

176   **BALANCING EXERCISES**

176   **DIVERGING STEPS IN A CIRCLE**
177   **WAGON WHEEL**

178   **SKILL DEVELOPMENT**

178   **FALL LINE SKATE**
178   **SKATE RACE**
179   **FALL LINE SKATE AND TURN**
179   **STEEP TRAVERSE, SKATE AND TURN**
179   **SKATE AND TURN**
179   **STEER THE INSIDE FOOT**
179   **EARLY WEIGHT TRANSFER**
180   **EXTENSION**

180   **LESSON PLAN**

180   **WARM YOUR BODY**
180   **RHYTHM AND REVIEW**
180   **DIRECTED FREE SKIING**
180   **SCHOOLWORK**
181   **MOUNTAIN PLAYGROUND**
182   **SLOW AND EASY**

182   **LESSON PLAN EXAMPLE**

CHAPTER 8
183   **DEEP SIDECUT CARVE**

185   **DEEP SIDECUT TECHNIQUE**

185   **BALANCE POINT**
186   **WIDE STANCE**
187   **TWO SKIS**
187   **BODY ANGLES**
188   **INSIDE SKI LEAD**
188   **TURN SHAPE**

189   **DIRECT CARVE PROGRESSION**

189   **TRAVERSE POSITION**
189   **TRAVERSE USING SIDECUT**

190   **TRAVERSE EXERCISES**

191   **TURN COMPLETION**

191   **EDGE CHANGE**

193   **LINK CARVED TURNS**

194   **MILES**

195   **DIAGONAL DESCENT**

195   **ROUND ARC**

197   **INCREASE SPEED**

199   **DYNAMIC CARVED TURNS**

201   **BEND AND EXTEND TURNS**

202   **DYNAMIC RETRACTION TURN**

203   **PULL FEET BACK**

204   **DYNAMIC SHORT RADIUS TURNS**

206   **REVERSE 180 TURN**

207   **MEDLEY**

207   **LESSON PLAN**

207   **WARM YOUR BODY**

207   **RHYTHM AND REVIEW**

208   **DIRECTED FREE SKIING**

208   **SCHOOLWORK**

208   **MOUNTAIN PLAYGROUND**

209   **SLOW AND EASY**

209   **LESSON PLAN EXAMPLE**

CHAPTER 9

211   **ON THE SNOW WARM-UP**

212   **WARM-UP EXERCISES**

212   **RUN IN PLACE**

212   **KNEE LIFT**

213   **SIDE STEP OVER POLE**

213   **ONE SKI SCOOTER**

214   **JUMP IN PLACE**

214   **JUMPING JACKS**

214   **KNEE TO ELBOW**

215   **DOWNHILL RACER**

215   **STRETCHING EXERCISES**

215   **HEAD MOVEMENT**

215   **HEAD LEAN**

216   **ARM CIRCLES**

216   **ARM CIRCLE VARIATION**

217   **ARM ROUTINE**

217   **HIP CIRCLES**

217   **SIDE STRETCH**

218   **TWISTING MOVEMENTS**

218   **CALF STRETCH**

219   **INSIDE LEG STRETCH**

219   **TAIL STRETCH**

219   **TIP STRETCH**

CHAPTER 10
221   **PERCEPTUAL SKILLS**

222   **VISUAL PERCEPTION**

222   **NOTICE OBJECTS**

222   **READ TERRAIN**

223   **LOOK AHEAD**

224   **IMAGERY**

224   **TACTILE AND VISUAL PERCEPTION**

224   **JUDGING SPEED**

224   **REGULATING SPEED**

225   **JUDGING DISTANCE**

225   **MAXIMIZING SPEED**

226   **FREE-SKI/COURSE**

226   **AUDITORY PERCEPTION**

226   **VERBAL CUES**

226   **LISTEN TO SKI SOUNDS**

227   *THE MOUNTAIN PLAYGROUND*

229   **GLOSSARY**

APPENDIX I
235   **CORRECTING ERRORS**

235   **COMMON ERRORS**

235   **LEANING BACK**
236   **BENDING FORWARD**
237   **NARROW STANCE**
237   **ARM POSITION**
238   **POLE ACTION**
239   **LOOKING DOWN**
240   **STIFF OUTSIDE LEG**
240   **UPPER BODY ROTATION**
241   **BANKING**
242   **EXCESSIVE WEIGHT ON THE INSIDE SKI**
242   **INSIDE SKI RAISED**
243   **RAILING**

APPENDIX II
244   **EQUIPMENT**

244   **SKIS**

244   **FLEX**
244   **SIZE**

245   **DEEP SIDECUT SKIS**

245   **SIDECUT RADIUS**

246   **WIDTH AT WAIST**

246   **SOFT FLEX**

246   **STABILITY**

247   **BENEFITS FOR BEGINNERS**

247   **BENEFITS FOR INTERMEDIATES**

247   **BENEFITS FOR EXPERTS**

247   **BENEFITS FOR RACERS**

248   **EDGE BEVEL**

248   **BOOTS**

248   **STANCE**

249   **SIZE**

249   **FLEX**

250   **CARVING BOOTS**

250   **BINDINGS**

251   **UNDER-BINDING PLATES**

251   **POLES**

251   **POLE LENGTH**

251   **POLE GRIP**

252   **GOGGLES**

252   **HELMETS**

252   **FEATURES**

253   **FIT AND SIZE**

254   **LEG ALIGNMENT**

255   **FOOT SUPPORT**

255   **UPPER CUFF ADJUSTMENT**

256   **CANTS**

APPENDIX III

257   **MODEL OF SKI**

APPENDIX IV

258   **LESSON PLAN WORKSHEET**

259   **INDEX**

265   **ABOUT THE AUTHOR**
265   **ABOUT THE PHOTOGRAPHER**
266   **THE TURNING POINT SKI FOUNDATION**
267   **ABOUT THE DEMONSTRATORS**

269   **EQUIPMENT INFORMATION**
270   **ORDERING INFORMATION**

271   *CLOSING NARRATIVE* ❋

AUTHOR'S NOTE

I would like to express my gratitude to Alan Schönberger for taking my thoughts, ideas and writings and shaping them into this book. He has provided much more than the monumental responsibilities of photographer, publisher and designer of this book. From his deep knowledge and abilities as a technical skier, ski teacher and artist, he has contributed to every aspect of the book.

Alan has approached this book in the same style that earned him a skiing World Championship, and in the same way he prepares for a theatre performance—with an intense focus that is driven by detail and a deep determination to do a better job than thought possible. He has a passion and a gift for making something as good as it could ever be. In every mountain, he sees an opportunity rather than an obstacle.

I wish to express heartfelt thanks to my father, Daniel Post. He has been the technical advisor of my work since my school days. At the mention of a difficult homework assignment, we would sit down at his desk. He would open a drawer and take out a pad of white paper and three or four freshly sharpened pencils. Recently, I sat at my computer ready to discuss revisions with my father. His first comment was, "Why don't you make a print-out and then we'll get started." I moved to my desk, print-out in hand, a pad of white paper and four newly sharpened pencils.

I greatly appreciate the effort and contribution made by Jay Evans. As the principal demonstrator, he displayed not only precision of movement, but the excitement, athleticism and beauty of skiing as well. During the process of working on this book, I was often reminded of Jay's true qualities, not only as a talented skier but as a superb person. His thoughts and ideas have helped to shape this book.

I would also like to thank Emily Anhalt, Dick Deming, Richard Mirrick, Scott Nyman, Annette E. Gras, Martin Olson, John Peppler, and Scott Smith who reviewed my work with care. Also, Mike Porter and Dave Mannetter for the insight they provided at the PSIA National Academy and Peter G. Ifju for his technical drawing of *Model the Ski.*

I am grateful

–to demonstrators, Steve Olwin and Tony Russo, who have contributed more than skiing expertise.

–to Kerry Weisman and the Communications Department of Keystone, Breckenridge and Arapahoe Basin for their support of our work.

–to Alan Henceroth and the Arapahoe Basin Ski Patrol who enabled us to work efficiently.

–to the Professional Ski Instructors of America Northwest and Rocky Mountain divisions' Education Foundations for their support, and for the opportunity to share my knowledge as an instructor and coach with the members of my profession.

–to Charlie Adams for his contribution on behalf of *Skis Dynastar,* to Marc Hauser and Dennis Leedom of *Boeri Sport USA*, to Hank Tauber of *Marker* ski bindings, Lisa Wilcox of *Bolle* goggles, and Hugh Schure and Greg McCreery of *Phenix* skiwear.

Special thanks to Brad, Randi and Will Foster for their patience, understanding and smiles. ❊

ARAPAHOE BASIN RESORT

Dan Rogers cared tremendously about our project and he went to great effort to help us.

Arapahoe Basin exceeds my childhood ski area in size, variety of terrain, powder days and scenic views. Yet it has a quality that is reminiscent of my home area and the ways of the past. I have become endeared to Arapahoe Basin because of the people I have met. It seems as though their friendliness is a gift the mountain has given them, a gift they want to share. There is a tremendous respect for the mountain—for its quiet beauty, and for, at times, its fierce expression. Nature's elements often dictate the procedure for the day.

For five years, we have come to Arapahoe Basin in the springtime. We have worked closely with the ski patrol staff. Their support on the mountain has made our extensive photographic desires possible. Many a time have they provided early morning snowmobile rides up the mountain, and endless rides back up to the top of *Sundance* to keep our photo shoot moving.

We would especially like to thank Alan Henceroth, Kerry Weisman, Dan Rogers and Leif Borgeson for their genuine interest in our work. ❊

Our mountain playground, Arapahoe Basin.

FOREWORD

Mike Porter
Ski School Director, Vail/Beaver Creek Ski School
Member, PSIA National Steering Committee
Former Head Coach, PSIA National Demonstration Team

Our sport is in the midst of a spirited and exciting revolution. New ski shapes, carving boots and new teaching approaches shorten the learning curve for the entry-level skier and promise intermediate and advanced skiers greater opportunities for improving their performance.

New equipment and new techniques have the potential to enhance every skier's performance and enjoyment. But, until now, no one has provided a complete technical guide for implementing the new developments in the sport. *Skiing and the Art of Carving* is not only the first book on how to maximize performance with today's equipment, it is also the definitive book on the subject.

Ellen Post Foster is an accomplished skier, a gifted ski teacher and a consummate learner. She is one of those rare individuals who can truly understand the characteristics of ski equipment and quickly feel and sense the new opportunities that will enhance performance. At the same time, Ellen has the unique ability to share this insight and guide others along the path of individual improvement. She takes the mystery out of learning.

What always fascinates me about Ellen's books is the complete scope of the material covered and the degree of detail addressed. And yet, each book is so clear and easy to follow that I want to go out and try it. Whatever your learning style preference—thinker, doer, watcher or feeler—you will receive a personalized game plan for ongoing improvement.

The design of each chapter in *Skiing and the Art of Carving* is unique and innovative. The mechanical focus is developed in a clear manner with excellent detailed photographs to reinforce the concept. Each chapter presents a broad list of appropriate exercises to guide you toward your outcome as well as self correcting tips to keep you from going astray. No matter what your ability level you can use this book as a step by step guide or as a reference piece to fine tune certain elements of your skiing.

Possibly the best attribute of this book is that it makes learning and improving fun. The variety of material covered allows you to personalize the lesson plan to suit your specific needs and to select exercises that you would like to do. Skiing is an exhilarating journey and Ellen is one of the best guides you could have. ❋

Rhythm

INTRODUCTION

When Tommy Moe stood at the top of the Downhill course at the Olympics, he was well prepared for the challenge. Years of concentrated effort had led to his extraordinary ability to carve turns at very high speeds. His technique was highly polished and he knew how to use it to his advantage. He had attained a level of performance in which well trained movements had become instinctive. When he charged out of the start, he was free on the race course, free to ski.

This book is all about developing and refining your technique. An accurate technique will allow you to ski intuitively and experience the powerful sensations that result. As your abilities increase, you gain the freedom to choose your "race course," whatever it might be.

Learning the *art* of carving is a process, a journey that leads to the highest level of skiing. It takes study, practice and observation to reach the level you aspire to attain. Miles of skiing and concentration on the *Art* of Carving will help you to acquire the knowledge, movement patterns and abilities for advancing your skills to meet the challenges of the mountain. ❋

DIRECTED FREE SKIING

I encountered the concept of "directed free skiing" when I was a young member of a Junior Demonstration Team. We worked constantly on our skiing—with our coach, with each other and by ourselves. We took notes, compared notes, and helped each other as we explored technique. Whether skiing through the glade, practicing hop turns on glare ice, or performing "final form parallel turns," we never lost an opportunity to practice.

This experience helped to shape my understanding of directed free skiing. I realized the importance of skiing with a focus, a direction in mind in order to promote improvement. The material in this book is designed to help you determine your personal direction. The self discipline of directed free skiing can help you take an active role in your own development. ❋

THE MOUNTAIN PLAYGROUND

It is exciting to acquire and refine skills, and to apply your abilities to ever-changing terrain. The mountain, like a gigantic playground, provides you with endless movement possibilities and places to explore. It takes a tremendous amount of time and experience to be able to adapt instinctively to terrain and snow conditions.

Terrain features and changeable snow conditions make every run a new experience. This creates a sense of adventure that contributes greatly to the excitement of skiing. Learning is fun in a playful environment.

My Junior Demonstration Team of years past had a reputation for the extraordinary technical abilities of its members, whose skiing was comparable to that of instructors rather than other children. I remember that we took great pride in being part of this team, but even more, we delighted in the fun we had on the mountain playground. ❄

CARVING

This book includes a multitude of exercises and progressions which establish a well-rounded performance leading to carving. "Carving" and "carve" are the terms used to describe a skier's ability to leave narrow, curved tracks in the snow. Most skiers aspire to accomplish carving since it offers the most efficient and consistent way to control direction, speed and stability. The very best skiers, whether they are World Cup racers or all-mountain skiers, strive to hone their skills in order to carve turns most effectively. ❄

DEEP SIDECUT SKIS

It is an exciting time in ski design with the emergence of deep sidecut skis. Truly a momentous change is taking place. New design and performance elements will likely have a powerful effect on all skiers. This is a sudden change, a change that can bring us closer to the paradigm of the elite ski racer. Deep sidecut skis provide an advantage that is comparable to the success of the wide body tennis racquet. In terms of skiing, carving has become less elusive and more accessible to all skiers, given the proper technique. We have found many skiers of deep sidecut skis have not tapped the ski's enormous potential. Let this book help you experience all of the advantages deep sidecut skis have to offer. ❄

HOW TO USE THIS BOOK

This book can help you take command of your development as a skier. You can learn what you need to practice, and how to add constructive focus to each run down the mountain.

This book can be used in a multitude of ways. If you are a beginning skier, it provides a step-by-step progression from which you can learn to ski. If you have reached a plateau, you may chose to determine your level of ability and proceed from there. If you have difficulties in certain situations, you may prefer to address them directly. Or, you may want to learn about skiing on deep sidecut skis. Whatever your intent, the material is here in this book to help you learn.

We feel strongly that the best way to reach your potential is to start at the beginning of the book. If you review each exercise and maneuver with attention to precision and accuracy, your foundation will become extremely solid and well-rounded. Any weaknesses you may discover will be addressed at a basic level where they are easiest to correct. This is really important, so we encourage you to sit by the fire, sip hot cocoa, and read in anticipation of an exciting day of skiing. ❄

LESSON PLANNING

This book contains a great deal of information and numerous exercises and progressions. You will find it easy to find your way through the material by following the lesson plans. Chapters 2–8 include a lesson plan format that you can personalize to meet your needs. Also, a sample lesson plan is provided. Each lesson plan includes the elements of warm-up, review, directed free skiing and schoolwork, all of which lead to the excitement of the mountain playground.

We would also encourage you to take a lesson from a professional. The ultimate experience would be to work closely with a professional ski instructor or coach in conjunction with this book. Ask, "Am I doing this maneuver correctly?" A professional can help recognize your errors and provide important feedback regarding your performance. Share your direction and goals with him/her. Together, you and your instructor or coach can use the material in this book to provide continuity to your development. He or she can ensure that you stay on course. ❈

OVERVIEW

Following is an overview of the content and layout of *Skiing and the* Art *of Carving*. The chapters consist of:

Chapter 1   A Curved Path
Chapter 2   Developing Balance
Chapter 3   Turning in a Wedge
Chapter 4   Parallel Turns
Chapter 5   Dynamic Skiing
Chapter 6   Quick Turns
Chapter 7   Step Turns
Chapter 8   Deep Sidecut Carve
Chapter 9   On the Snow Warm-up
Chapter 10 Perceptual Skills

A Curved Path presents a description of the functional and technical aspects of a carved turn and an explanation of the relationship between ski design and carved turns. A model is used to illustrate correct ski action.

Together, Chapters 2 through 7 provide a progression that begins with basic maneuvers and builds to expert skiing. These chapters cover balance and skill development exercises, ski pole action, turn shape and terrain and snow conditions. At the end of each chapter, guidelines are given to help you design a personal lesson plan. A lesson plan example is also provided.

Deep Sidecut Carve specifically addresses the needs of experienced skiers who ski on deep sidecut skis. It includes the primary changes in technique that allow you to use the design of the ski. A *Direct Carve Progression* provides a detailed progression that can help you carve turns most effectively.

On the Snow Warm-up provides exercises to warm and stretch the body at the start of each day or to warm-up during a cold day.

Perceptual Skills explains how sensory information provides essential cues about terrain, snow conditions, speed, and distances.

A *Glossary* of terms follows the last chapter. It will help you to locate definitions easily. The first time that a word from the *Glossary* appears in the text, it is printed in italics.

Appendix I covers *Correcting Errors*, in which incorrect actions are described, negative outcomes are identified, and a plan for improvement is given.

Appendix II, Equipment, provides information that pertains to selecting equipment; traditional or deep sidecut skis, boots, bindings, under-binding plates, poles, goggles and helmets. In addition, this section covers leg alignment and canting.

Appendix III contains a pattern of a ski that can be copied and used to illustrate the concept of carving as described in *Model the Ski,* Chapter 1, *A Curved Path.*

Appendix IV provides a *Lesson Plan Worksheet* for you to copy and use. ❄

FREE CARVE SKIING VIDEO

Information about the video, *Free Carve Skiing*, (based on this book) and other books by the *Turning Point Ski Foundation* is given under *Ordering Information* at the back of the book. ❄

LESSON PLANNING

Quiet power

LESSON PLANNING

A lesson plan can help you work toward a long-term goal and add constructive focus to each run down the hill. By determining objectives, you establish a clear direction for your work. The following outline provides a framework for the design of a lesson plan. At the end of each of Chapters 2–8, specific information is given for the purpose of designing a lesson plan that is relevant to the material within each chapter. After you read the following description, turn to *Lesson Plan* at the end of any chapter to see how the following information is applied.

To design your lesson plan, you can copy and fill in the *Lesson Plan Worksheet* that is provided in *Appendix IV*. Take your notes in your pocket to review in the lodge or on the chairlift.

DAILY LESSON PLAN. The general plan for a day of skiing includes:

- (a) Warm Your Body
- (b) Rhythm and Review
- (c) Directed Free Skiing
- (d) Schoolwork
- (e) Mountain Playground
- (f) Slow and Easy

WARM YOUR BODY. Start each day with a warm-up, even if your lesson plan is altered because of terrain, weather and snow conditions, or time constraints. When your body is warm, you can perform movements with better balance and coordination. Your muscles need to be warm to achieve optimal performance and avoid injury. Activities such as jogging in place will raise your heart rate, increase your body temperature and prepare your muscles and joints for strenuous activity.

When you feel warm, begin stretching exercises to help guard against muscle, tendon and ligament strains and sprains. Refer to *On-Snow Exercises* for ideas of exercises that will help warm and stretch your body. Make note of the exercises you would like to include in your lesson plan. It is helpful to establish a set routine that you can repeat each morning.

During the day, return to warm-up exercises after a break or whenever you are cold.

RHYTHM AND REVIEW. It is reassuring to feel comfortable on your skis right away. To achieve this, start your day with rhythmic turns on smooth terrain. Rhythmic turns allow you to focus on feelings and sensations in consistent surroundings. Select a speed and turn size that feels best. Consider starting at a slow speed on gentle terrain. World Champion, Ingemar Stenmark skied as slowly as he possibly could to warm-up while his competitors skied by him at race speeds. Stenmark believed it is more difficult to ski precisely at slow speeds, and by doing so, his turns would be more accurate when he increased his speed just before a race.

Keep a checklist of key elements that, when reviewed, help you achieve your best turns. The list may include feeling weight along the inside of your foot to stay balanced on the outside ski, using wrist action to plant your pole, or looking ahead.

DIRECTED FREE SKIING. Free-ski with a specific objective in mind to improve your performance. Stay focused on accomplishing one task at a time. From the consistent experience in *Rhythm and Review*, progress to variable terrain as you free ski on the mountain. Also, vary the size and speed of your turns, as you work toward a specific goal. Your objective may be to keep your feet apart, maintain contact between your lower leg and the front of your boot, or link turns without traverses.

SCHOOLWORK. This is the time to use specific exercises to develop or refine a skill, or correct a problem. Work toward performing movements with precision, improving body awareness, and learning new movements. Also:

(a) Use exercises with technical goals in mind.

(b) Select exercises that are appropriate for your ability level.

(c) Use the skill, drill, hill formula. The skill is what you would like to learn. The drill is the situation you create to encourage learning. The hill is the appropriate terrain for success.

(d) Practice an exercise sufficiently. It takes continual practice, in different situations, to refine a skill. Practicing an exercise once during each run will lead to greater success than practicing once during the entire day.

(e) Put the same effort into performing an exercise with precision as you put into your best turns.

(f) Relate exercises back to actual skiing.

To select specific exercises, refer to the listing at the end of each chapter, or refer to a *Corrective Plan* in *Appendix I*. Make notes the night before concerning what you want to achieve and the exercises you will use. Be careful not to do too much in one day. Take the time to be thorough with each exercise so that it is most effective.

MOUNTAIN PLAYGROUND. Apply your turns to varied, and increasingly more difficult, terrain and snow conditions. The mountain is like a gigantic playground. It provides skiers with endless movement possibilities and places to explore. Terrain features and changeable snow conditions make every run a new experience. It takes a tremendous amount of time and practice to be able to adapt spontaneously to the mountain playground.

Plan where you will ski and add these places to your notes.

SLOW AND EASY. At the end of the day, ski on smooth slopes to relax, especially if you are feeling tired. It may be helpful to take "mindless" runs after a day of focused skiing. ✳

THE JOURNEY

As you learn and refine new skills and apply your abilities to the mountain playground, you will undoubtedly experience many adventures. Exciting and memorable moments will mark your journey. You are embarking on an exploration that is not unlike that of an artist. First, one must have a firm technical foundation in his or her discipline, and this will consist of highly developed basic skills. Only then is an artist or athlete liberated to create or perform freely without constraints. ❄

Tommy Moe, Olympic Gold Medalist

One goes out onstage with a well-prepared technique, a knowledge of how to present that technique in its most refined form. But beyond that, what counts is the ability to be free on the stage, to dance.

Mikhail Baryshnikov

Deep carve

CHAPTER 1:
A CURVED PATH

This chapter introduces fundamental concepts related to carved turns. Subsequent chapters provide the practical information that leads to carving, culminating in Chapter 8, *Deep Sidecut Carve*. In *A Curved Path*, the relationship between ski design and carved turns is explained. This information is important for beginning and experienced skiers alike. ❄

Have you noticed? The best skiers raise the smallest plume of snow behind their skis (Figure 1.1). Those that splash great flurries of snow are not as proficient. It is just like the best swimmers—those who splash the least are the best.

The secret is carved turns. Carved turns mark the path to efficient, effective and graceful skiing. They allow you to maneuver along a desired path, to control speed, direction and stability, and to enjoy precise skiing.

A carved turn occurs when an *edged* ski travels through a curved path, or *arc*, without *slipping* or *skidding*. The result is a

FIGURE 1.1
Little snow plumes behind this ski racer as he carves his way through a race course.

precise and efficient change of direction. The size, shape and extent of the path determine how fast you descend a slope.

Multiple movement patterns are necessary to ski arcs most effectively. You must actively tip both skis onto corresponding edges and align your body accordingly to stay in balance. The *outside ski* of a turn plays a dominate role in controlling the arc of the turn. To balance on the outside ski, you must concentrate your weight along its inside edge (FIGURE 1.2).

SKI DESIGN. The shape and flexibility of the ski is designed to optimize carved turns. The front (tip) and back (tail) of the ski are broader than the center (waist); the resultant curve along the length of the ski is called *sidecut*. The roundness, or shape of the turn, is determined by the design of the ski, also. Primary design factors include flex, sidecut, length and torsional rigidity.

Sidecut is measured by the differences in width of a ski at the tip, tail and waist (FIGURE 1.3 and FIGURE 1.4). In general, the more

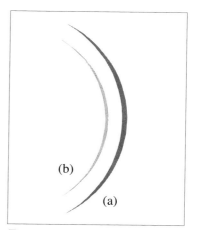

FIGURE 1.2

The outside ski (a) is farther from the center of the turn than the inside ski (b).

FIGURE 1.3

The shape of the tip (left) of a deep sidecut ski and a traditional ski.

FIGURE 1.4

The shape of the tail (right) of a deep sidecut ski and a traditional ski.

FIGURE 1.5

Flexing a ski into an arc (left).

FIGURE 1.6

Twisting only the tip of a ski to show the torsional component of ski design (right).

sidecut a ski has, the sharper it will turn.

Flex is determined by the amount of force that is necessary to bend a ski into an arc (FIGURE 1.5). A softer ski will bend into a deeper arc more easily than a comparatively stiffer ski.

Length affects the ease of turning and stability of a ski. In general, a shorter length ski is easier to turn, but a relatively longer ski is more stable at high speeds. Also, a shorter ski will turn in a tighter arc compared to a longer ski of the same sidecut.

Torsional rigidity refers to the ability of a ski to resist twisting (FIGURE 1.6). A torsionally rigid ski tends to hold an arc more effectively. When the ski twists, the angle of the edge in the snow changes, thus altering the curved path of the ski.

BEND THE SKI. Forces generated by body weight are responsible for making a ski bend. Imagine a block under the tip and tail of your ski (FIGURE 1.7). When you stand on the ski, your body weight bends the ski into an arc. When the ski is tipped on edge,

FIGURE 1.7
Standing on blocks illustrates the curve of a weighted ski.

that arc is pressed into the snow, scribing a curved path.

TIP THE SKI. A weighted ski must be tipped on edge to turn. Movement of the body toward the center of the turn inclines the legs and tips the skis on edge. An additional tipping movement of the foot concentrates the body force closer to the inside edge of the foot, as indicated by the shaded zone in the figure (FIGURE 1.8). This is the condition that makes it easiest to hold the ski on edge throughout the turn.

Actually, the ski boot restricts the tipping movement of the foot, and the motion illustrated in the diagram is exaggerated. Nevertheless, the effort concentrates the force along the edge of the foot/ski where it is most effective.

Try the following exercises as described in the photo captions to study the movement and sensation of tipping the foot (FIGURE 1.9, 1.10 and 1.11).

A CARVED TURN. When the skis are used accurately, a *carved turn* occurs. Pure *carving* is accomplished by tipping (angulating) and weighting the ski so that it bends into a circular arc. The edge of the ski moves along a corresponding circular arc to form a

FIGURE 1.8

The muscle action that attempts to tip the foot at the ankle concentrates force along the edge of the foot.

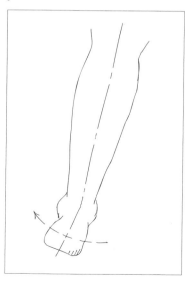

curved track in the snow. In this way, the ski travels forward through the arc of the turn without skidding sideways. Carving maintains your speed, whereas skidding decreases speed. With a carved turn, the speed of descent is controlled by the amount of direction change that occurs. Ski through a large segment of an arc (complete your turn more) to reduce speed. Ski through a smaller segment of the same arc to increase speed (FIGURE 1.12).

MODEL THE SKI. The following demonstration illustrates the characteristics of a ski in relation to a carved turn (FIGURE 1.13). It is such a useful lesson that we should all perform the demonstration. It is easy and striking.

(1) Cut out the exaggerated shape of a ski, like the diagram in the figure. Cut it from thin cardboard or an index card. Bend the ski tip upwards.

(2) Gently curve the model into a circular arc by pulling it through your fingers.

(3) Place the model on a flat surface and tip it on edge.

Notice that the edge of the ski rests on the surface along a circular arc. If the surface was snow, the edge would cut into the snow to form a shallow groove in the form of a circular arc. As the ski moves forward it would continue in the arc. The groove would be like a circular track.

We see that the reason for the sidecut is to cause the ski to turn in a smooth arc, without slipping or skidding in the track. We see, too, that the *radius* of the turn depends upon how much the ski is bent by the forces exerted on the skis by the skier. The model also shows the importance of torsional rigidity. Twist the tip to partially flatten it on the snow. The edge engages the snow along a new arc which means the ski cannot track in a constant radius. Some skidding will occur.

FIGURE 1.9

Lean against a support and incline your lower body toward the support.

FIGURE 1.10 (Bottom left)

Lift your outside foot and roll your foot to the outside (left).

FIGURE 1.11 (Bottom right)

Continue to tip your foot as you set it on the ground. Feel how concentrated your weight is along the inside edge of your foot. This action distributes weight along the inside edge of the ski (right).

TERMINOLOGY. The following terms distinguish carving from other ways to cross the surface of the snow.

(a) Slide—forward travel of a flat ski.

(b) Slip—sideways travel of a flat ski.

(c) Pivot—twisting or rotating a flat ski about a vertical axis without changing the skier's direction of travel.

(d) Skid—sideways travel on an angulated ski that changes the skier's direction. In a skidded turn, a pivot of an insufficiently angulated ski occurs.

A STEERED TURN. *Steering* occurs when an additional torque is applied by the leg to change the path of the ski from the path of pure carving. This twisting force causes a *pivoting* action, such that steering always adds a pivoting or skidding motion to the ski. The track is no longer a sharp impression of the angulated ski, but rather, it is a broader swath of disturbed snow caused by the skidding action.

NEW TECHNOLOGY. The technology behind ski design is in an exciting state of development. Skis sporting a deeper sidecut have become the present rage, with good cause. Deep sidecut skis make it easier to carve turns. The wonderful sensations that accompany slicing cleanly through the snow are addictive. It is this excitement that motivates the pursuit of further skills.

Although the name refers to sidecut in particular, all design characteristics of deep sidecut skis have been re-engineered. Deep sidecut skis are usually made to be skied in shorter lengths, typically ten centimeters less than traditional skis. Some skis with extreme sidecut are intended to be used in even shorter lengths. With new blueprints and materials, these skis are surprisingly stable. Flex, torsional rigidity and overall width have also been changed accordingly to enhance performance.

The progression in Chapter 8, *Deep Sidecut Carve*, helps you make the transition from traditional skis to most effective use of deep sidecut skis. ❇

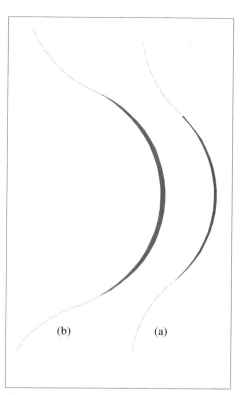

(b)   (a)

FIGURE 1.12

When you ski a smaller segment (a) of the circular arc of a carved turn, there is less direction change and, therefore, the speed is greater than when you ski a larger segment of the arc (b).

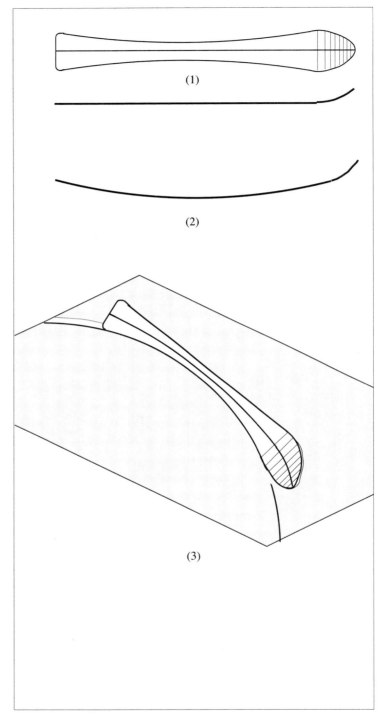

(1)

(2)

(3)

FIGURE 1.13
This figure illustrates how to model a carving turn on any smooth surface. A larger pattern of the ski (1) can be found in Appendix III. Copy the larger pattern to try this exercise.

CHAPTER 2: DEVELOPING BALANCE

Flurry

Skier, Liz Golting

CHAPTER 2:
DEVELOPING BALANCE

Being in balance is crucial at every level of skiing. A balanced position provides the basis for wedge turns and dynamic carved turns alike.

Start with this chapter if you are beginning to learn to ski. If you are an experienced skier, scan this chapter to review the correct body position at your current level. Numerous exercises are given for the beginner. These instructions and exercises apply for both traditional skis and deep sidecut skis. With deep sidecut skis, the optimum stance is slightly modified, as noted in the text. ❋

BALANCED STANCE

FIGURE 2.1

When in balance, you can lift your entire ski (left).

FIGURE 2.2

Bending forward at the hips restricts leg movement (right).

BODY POSITION. Skiing is a demanding sport in that the "playing field" constantly changes. The snow conditions, the irregular surface, and the pitch of the hill can vary greatly even from turn to turn. In this changeable environment, a balanced position is critical to ski where you desire, at a speed that is comfortable.

To attain a *balanced stance*, start in a fairly tall position. Stand with your feet comfortably apart in an *open stance* for balance and stability. Make sure your skis are parallel, pointing in the same direction. Use your bone structure and not muscular strength to support your weight. Slightly bend your ankles, knees, hips and

spinal column. A straight, stiff back is not recommended. Instead, round your lower back slightly while tightening your stomach muscles gently. Keep your arms in front of your body to help with balance. Also for balancing purposes, your hands should be positioned several inches further apart than the width of your body. Look ahead to aid balance and to see upcoming terrain and snow conditions.

PRACTICE THE STANCE. Wear your ski boots to do the following exercises.

(a) Stand straight, with your weight balanced over the center of your feet. Bend slightly at the ankle, knee and hip joints, so that your straight back moves purely downward, i.e., without moving forward or backward. Now, pull in your stomach muscles, and slightly round your lower back. Do not move your shoulders forward or backward. This sequence aligns your body into the recommended balanced stance.

(b) Compare bending forward at the hips with a relatively straight back to rounding your lower back. It is helpful to look in a mirror to see if your movements are correct.

(c) Note that you have the freedom to lift your whole ski off the snow when you are in a balanced stance (Figure 2.1). When you bend forward at the hips, your leg movements become restricted (Figure 2.2). Only the tail of the ski can be lifted from this position. Test your body position to see if you can lift your whole ski while staying in balance over the center of your weighted foot.

BALANCE POINT. The *balance point* is located at the middle of the sole of your foot. This point corresponds to the most efficient location to apply downward force to a ski. Skis are designed to bend into a circular arc when forces are applied at this point. The sensory feedback you receive from your feet is very important for making adjustments to improve balance. Pay attention to the feelings, or feedback ("feetback"), you get from your feet in order to maintain your weight over the balance point (FIGURES 2.3, 2.4 and 2.5).

FIGURE 2.3
Weight too far forward (top).

FIGURE 2.4
Weight too far back (middle).

FIGURE 2.5
A balanced position (bottom).

FIGURE 2.6

NOTES FOR DEEP SIDECUT SKIS. Stand in a slightly wider stance on deep sidecut skis to compensate for the added width of the skis. Deep sidecut skis are designed to be skied with more edge angle and more flex than traditional skis. These characteristics necessitate a wider stance.

COMMON MISTAKES. It is difficult to ski if you are sitting back, if your leg joints are kept rigid, if you are bent forward at the hips or waist, or if your stance is too low. In addition to misplaced force on the skis, these incorrect stances demand muscular exertion which is tiresome and stressful. ✳

FIGURE 2.7
Walk around objects to get used to being in ski boots.

FIRST MOVEMENTS

WALKING. Walk in your ski boots before you put on your skis (FIGURE 2.7). This will help you find your balance and feel your boots flex as you bend your ankles. Randomly place objects such as books or paper cups on your living room floor. Walk around the objects. Then, walk on the snow to experience a slippery surface.

GETTING UP FROM A FALL. When you fall, move your skis until they point across the hill. This will keep you from sliding as you begin to stand. Place your downhill hand on top of both pole grips and press the tips of your poles into the snow next to your uphill hip. Place your uphill hand on the baskets of the poles and push upward. Pull down with the hand that is holding both grips. In this way, raise your body directly above the tails of your skis. Continue to push with your poles as you straighten your body (FIGURES 2.8 a, b, c).

FIGURES 2.8 a, b, c
Use your poles to help you get up on two skis.

FIGURES 2.9 a, b, c

It is easier to get up when one ski is off.

If you have difficulty getting up in this way, take one ski off (FIGURES 2.9 a, b, c). This is the same method that is used when a ski comes off in a fall. Maneuver around until your ski is downhill from your free leg. First, point your ski across the hill, and then, kneel onto your uphill knee. Use your poles as previously described to raise onto your foot in order to stand.

SLIDING STEPS. Slide one ski ahead, and then the other, to move forward (FIGURE 2.10). As you slide your skis, your body weight shifts from one foot to the other. Use your poles to assist with balancing. Bring one arm forward as you advance the opposite leg in a natural walking movement.

FIGURE 2.10

Sliding steps are much like walking, but without lifting your feet.

LIFT A SKI. Balancing on one ski is helpful for learning to shift weight (FIGURE 2.11). Use your ski poles to help you balance as you stand on one leg. Lift your other leg at the knee to raise your ski off the snow.

SIDESTEP. To step up the hill, start with your skis pointing across the hill (FIGURE 2.12). Use your ski poles for support as you step sideways. Tip your skis onto their uphill edges to grip the snow as you climb.

FIGURE 2.11

Practice balancing on one ski.

WALK AROUND OBJECTS. Walking around objects is helpful for learning to maneuver on long skis (FIGURE 2.13). Use objects such as twigs or paper cups. Take small steps to pivot around the tips or tails of your skis to turn around the objects. Use your ski poles to maintain balance.

FIGURE 2.12

Sidestepping up the hill feels much like walking up a staircase sideways.

FIGURE 2.13

Walk around objects to get used to maneuvering on skis.

STEP OVER OBJECTS. Stepping movements are helpful to become comfortable with the length and weight of a ski (FIGURE 2.14). Step over the objects in your homemade obstacle course to improve your balance on one ski and your ability to shift weight.

ONE SKI SCOOTER. This exercise is excellent for developing overall balance and for finding a centered stance. It is invaluable for learning to balance on the downhill ski of a traverse or the outside ski of a turn.

Take a ski off and walk around on one ski. Push off with your ski boot and glide on the ski (Figure 2.15). Scooter to a distant

FIGURE 2.14

Step over objects to practice moving your skis, considering their length.

object on flat terrain. Scooter around objects such as ski poles, cones, or Slalom poles, to develop balance. After feeling comfortable on either ski, try to scooter without using your ski poles. ❆

FIGURE 2.15
Push with your foot and glide on your ski.

BALANCING EXERCISES

FIGURE 2.16
Slide down the hill in a balanced stance.

SLIDE DOWNHILL. Slide straight down a very gentle slope that has a flat or slightly uphill runout (FIGURE 2.16). Assume a balanced stance that is characterized by:

(a) a fairly tall body position, supported by the skeleton

(b) joints that are slightly flexed

(c) feet that are comfortably apart and equally weighted

(d) hands that are in front of the body

(e) eyes that look ahead

(f) weight on the middle of the foot on traditional skis, on the ball of the foot on deep sidecut skis

BALANCE ROUTINE. As you slide down a hill, practice motions chosen from the following list. Resume a balanced stance between each movement. It is fun and challenging to expand your experiences by combining the movements into different routines (FIGURE 2.17).

(a) reach for the sky, touch the snow

(b) touch your right boot top with your glove; touch your left boot top

(c) march from foot to foot, sliding on one foot between each step

FIGURE 2.17
As you slide downhill, lift one ski and shuffle your feet.

(d) alternate sliding one ski forward as you pull the other foot
back in a shuffling manner

(e) lift one ski completely off the snow

(f) jump on both skis

(g) hop on one ski

(h) step sideways to a new line

STEP OVER POLES. The experience of stepping over poles requires balance and coordination, and introduces the skill of edging. You have to move off the edge of one ski and then the other to change direction or step over the poles.

Use ten poles to lay a course on flat terrain. Set the poles flat on the snow, pointing in random directions. Space the poles so that the ends are touching, or are no more than two meters apart. Maneuver to step over every pole. Then, try these variations:

(a) step over red poles only

(b) follow a leader over all the poles

(c) hop on one foot over every pole, walk between poles

(d) do the course without using ski poles ❄

CONTROL OF SPEED

WEDGE POSITION. You can control your speed on gentle terrain with a wedge (FIGURE 2.18 and FIGURE 2.19). To learn a wedge, start with a balanced stance on flat terrain. Keep the tips of your skis close together, but move the tails apart. Tip your skis onto their inside edges by concentrating your weight along the inside of your feet. The edges provide resistance against the surface of the snow to slow your descent. The degree of tipping is called the *edge angle*. When the edge angle increases, greater resistance occurs and speed decreases.

Make sure your weight is even on both skis and your upper body is centered between your skis. Stand over the center of your foot for traditional skis. Stand over the ball of your foot for *deep sidecut skis*.

JUMP TO A WEDGE POSITION. This exercise encourages an

FIGURE 2.18 and FIGURE 2.19

In a wedge position, ski tips are close and tails are apart. Maintain a balanced stance.

equal spreading action of the tails of the skis. Start in a balanced position on flat terrain with your ski poles planted firmly by your ski tips. Supported by your poles, jump and spread the tails of your skis apart. Land on the inside edges in a wedge position (FIGURES 2.20 a, b, c).

SLIDE IN A WEDGE. Start in a wedge facing straight down a very gentle slope that has a flat or slightly uphill runout (FIGURE 2.21). Hold yourself in place by increasing the edge angle. Then, slightly flatten your skis by moving your knees outward to achieve less edge angle and to slide downhill. If you do not start to move,

FIGURES 2.20 a, b, c

Spread your skis equally apart as you jump.

place the tips of your poles in the snow behind your boots and push with your poles. Then, place your arms in front of your body. Bend your elbows slightly. Hold your poles as pictured to encourage correct body position.

VARY WEDGE WIDTH. When you feel comfortable sliding down a hill, vary the width of your wedge. Try a narrower stance with less edge angle to glide faster (FIGURE 2.22). Try a wider stance with more edge angle to travel slower (FIGURE 2.23).

FIGURE 2.21
Keep your upper body steady.

WEDGE TO A STOP. From a narrow wedge, smoothly press the tails of your skis farther apart to come to a stop (FIGURE 2.24). As you widen your wedge, lower your body by gradually flexing at the ankle, knee, and torso. Make sure your knees aim and bend toward the tips of your skis and do not come together. Keep the tips of your skis close together as you spread the tails apart. As the wedge becomes wider, the edge angle will become steeper. Therefore, resistance against the snow will become greater and speed will decrease. Increase the width of the wedge until you come to a complete stop.

The edge angle of the skis should increase gradually in order to come to a stop smoothly. In contrast, a quick move to a steeply edged ski can cause the ski to catch in the snow and topple the skier.

FIGURE 2.22
Move down the hill in a narrow wedge (left).

FIGURE 2.23
Move down the hill in a wide wedge (right).

PARALLEL AND WEDGE POSITIONS. Alternate between parallel and wedge positions as you slide straight down a gentle slope (FIGURE 2.25).

Starting from a parallel position, bend your ankles, knees and torso as you spread the tails of your skis into a wedge (FIGURE 2.26). As your skis move farther away from the center of your body, the edge angle will increase, and you will slow down. Extend your body to flatten your edges and to pull your legs closer together into a parallel position. Your speed will increase.

Your weight should remain over the center of each foot. (Over the ball of your foot on deep sidecut skis.) Concentrate also on the feeling of weight acting along the inside of your foot. The ski will be edged less when your foot is flatter. The more the knee and foot are tipped toward the inside, the steeper the angle of the edge will be on the snow. ✿

FIGURE 2.24

Widening the wedge will increase the edge angle of the skis on the snow and bring you to a stop.

FIGURE 2.25

Alternate between parallel and wedge positions.

FIGURE 2.26
Gradually lower your stance as you widen your wedge.

LESSON PLAN

This first lesson plan is easy since the material is restricted to balancing movements and maneuvers preceding wedge turns. Therefore, it provides a good opportunity to experience the lesson planning process. Select the exercises or subjects from each category that you would like to practice. Make notes that you can take with you on the hill. Vary your lesson plan for subsequent days.

WARM YOUR BODY. Refer to Chapter 9, *On the Snow Warm-up* for descriptions of the following:

Warm-up Exercises:
   (a) *Run in Place*
   (b) *One Ski Scooter*
Stretching Exercises:
   (a) *Head Movement*
   (b) *Arm Circles*
   (c) *Arm Routine*
   (d) *Hip Circles*
   (e) *Side Stretch*
   (f) *Twisting Movements*
   (g) *Calf Stretch*

RHYTHM AND REVIEW. Repeatedly slide in a wedge and stop in a wedge on a very gentle slope. Focus on one of the following topics at a time.

Elements of a balanced stance:
  (a) fairly tall position
  (b) bend at the ankles, knees and hips
  (c) rounded lower back
  (d) arms in front of the body
  (e) look ahead
  (f) weight on the middle of the foot on traditional skis, on the ball of the foot on deep sidecut skis

Wedge position:
  (a) tips close and tails apart
  (b) bend knees toward the tips of the skis

Stop:
  (a) press the edged skis apart equally and smoothly to increase the width of the wedge and stop

DIRECTED FREE SKIING. Practice varying the width of the wedge and making the transition between parallel and wedge positions. Choose a focus from the following:
  (a) quiet upper body
  (b) lower the body to widen the wedge, raise the body to bring skis closer together
  (c) make movements gradual and smooth
  (d) practice looking ahead (see Notice Objects in Chapter 10, *Perceptual Skills*)

SCHOOLWORK. Select from these movement exercises:
  (a) *Walking*
  (b) *Sliding Steps*
  (c) *Lift a Ski*
  (d) *Sidestep*
  (e) *Walk Around Objects*
  (f) *Step Over Objects*

Select from these balancing exercises:
  (a) *Balance Routine*

(b) *Step Over Poles*

MOUNTAIN PLAYGROUND. Ski over uneven terrain.

SLOW AND EASY. Ski in a narrow, gliding wedge position.

LESSON PLAN EXAMPLE:

WARM YOUR BODY.
    (a) *Run in Place*
    (b) *Head Movement*
    (c) *Arm Circles*
    (d) *Hip Circles*
    (e) *Side Stretch*
    (f) *Twisting Movements*
    (g) *Calf Stretch*

RHYTHM AND REVIEW. Practice going from a wedge to a stop. Focus on the following:
    (a) arms in front of the body
    (b) bend knees toward the tips of the skis

DIRECTED FREE SKIING. Vary the width of the wedge. Work on:
    (a) quiet upper body
    (b) look ahead (see *Notice Objects* in Chapter 10, *Perceptual Skills*)

SCHOOLWORK.
    (a) *Sliding Steps*
    (b) *Sidestep*
    (c) *Balance Routine*

MOUNTAIN PLAYGROUND. Ski over uneven terrain.

SLOW AND EASY. Ski in a narrow, gliding wedge. ❈

CHAPTER 3: TURNING IN A WEDGE

Miles

CHAPTER 3:
TURNING IN A WEDGE

The skills that are developed in wedge turns establish a basic foundation for all levels of skiing. In this chapter, wedge turns on both traditional skis and deep sidecut skis are covered.

The descriptions and progressions in this chapter will help a beginning skier learn to turn competently. An experienced skier who has reached a plateau will find this chapter helpful since shortcomings become more obvious, and easier to correct, in a wedge turn. An experienced skier who converts to deep sidecut skis will find the wedge provides a stable position to feel the sensation of carving on the outside ski. Look for *NOTES FOR DEEP SIDE-CUT SKIS*.

TURN DESCRIPTION. In a wedge turn, maintain the wedge position throughout the turn; the tips of the skis are close together and the tails are apart. Start each turn with a slight rising motion combined with a steering of the skis into the turn. (To steer the legs and feet, apply a torque, or gradual pivoting force.) Gradually transfer your weight to the outside ski of the turn. Tip the outside ski on edge and increase the degree of tipping through the turn. When half the turn is completed, begin to lower your body by gradually flexing your ankle, knee, and torso. Face your upper body in the direction of the upcoming turn and continue to face that direction throughout the rest of the turn. Link rhythmic, round-shaped turns, maintaining the width of the wedge (FIGURE 3.1).

NOTES FOR DEEP SIDECUT SKIS. This description is appropriate for turns on traditional skis and deep sidecut skis. Although the design of a deep sidecut ski makes carving easier, it is necessary to achieve a broad experience that includes sideways as well as forward movement of a ski through a turn. This will prepare you for future demands of terrain, snow conditions and speed management. You may find that progress on deep sidecut skis happens more quickly and that you may be able to accomplish lower level maneuvers sooner. It is still necessary to devote sufficient time to each exercise to feel comfortable and competent in a variety of situations before moving to more difficult exercises and maneuvers. ❄

FIGURE 3.1
The skills that are developed in wedge turns establish a basic foundation for all levels of skiing.

SKILL DEVELOPMENT

FIGURE 3.2

The movement patterns in a wedge turn and a parallel turn are very similar. In this photograph, the leader is in a wedge position and the follower is in a parallel position. The primary difference is the position of the inside leg.

WEDGE/PARALLEL. The skills you learn at a wedge turn level are the same skills that are used in parallel turns (FIGURE 3.2). Therefore, it is important to learn the movements correctly from the very beginning.

UPPER BODY POSITION. The upper body can aid in balance or it can disturb balance through unnecessary movement. Keep a steady upper body and an active lower body as you ski (FIGURE 3.3). In turns close to the fall line, aim your upper body straight down the hill. Keep your arms in front of your body and your hands several inches wider than the width of your body. Look ahead to assist balance and to see upcoming terrain.

THE OUTSIDE SKI. The outside ski of a wedge turn controls the arc of the turn. To identify the outside ski, think of a turn as half of a circle. The ski that is farther away from the center of the circle is the outside ski of the turn. The ski that is closer to the center is the *inside ski*. (Review the diagram in *A Curved Path*, Chapter 1.)

At the beginning of a wedge turn, transfer your weight to the

FIGURE 3.3

The legs turn underneath a quiet upper body.

outside ski by moving your upper body sideways. This ski can be thought of as the "heavy" ski in comparison to the "light" inside ski. As you link turns, use verbal cues such as "right ski, left ski" to help transfer your weight to the appropriate outside ski.

FLEX AND EXTEND. For a beginning skier, rising and lowering movements of the body are helpful. They promote rhythm and the linking of turns, and they discourage a static or stiff body position. At a more advanced level of skiing, these vertical movements are replaced with lateral movements of the legs.

During the first half of the turn, rise by extending your ankles, knees and torso until your skis point straight down the hill (FIGURE 3.4). Then, bend by flexing your ankles, knees and torso during the second half of the turn until your downhill ski points across the hill. Flexing to lower the body occurs to reduce *pressure* on the skis.

FIGURE 3.4

From a low stance at the end of a turn, smoothly rise to a taller stance. Then, gradually lower your body through the completion of the turn. This movement is exaggerated in this photograph.

Otherwise, the skis can skid as pressure increases through this part of the turn. Flexion and extension movements of the body are slight and not deep. Rising and lowering should occur in a smooth wave of movement.

NOTE FOR DEEP SIDECUT SKIS. At the beginning of a turn on deep sidecut skis, extension of the outside leg occurs to weight and bend the outside ski. The body moves in a lateral direction, toward the inside of the turn, compared to vertically (on traditional skis), in which case both skis are weighted and steered.

THE INSIDE SKI. During a turn, the inside leg and ski is not heavily weighted. The ski is kept relatively flat on the snow and moves along the snow at an angle to the path of the outside ski. Its function is to provide a broad platform to catch the skier if he/she loses balance. The inside ski must be directed to coincide with the path of the outside ski. In the second half of a turn, the inside leg must bend sufficiently to compensate for its higher position on a hillside.

Use the inside ski to facilitate a smooth transition between turns. At the beginning of a turn, advance your inside ski slightly ahead of the outside ski. This *"lead ski"* action helps to transfer your weight to the outside ski. Also, it aligns your body in such a way that the tails of the skis are less apt to skid. In the *countered* body position that occurs, the outside hip is slightly back in relation to the inside hip.

CARVING. Carving requires more accuracy than steering. It is a more effective way to control speed, direction and stability. What really happens in a carved turn? When you transfer your weight to the outside ski, your body weight bends the ski into an arc. When the ski is tipped on edge, that arc is pressed into the snow, making

FIGURE 3.5

The outside ski travels forward in a circular arc, and does not skid outside the arc.

a carved turn (FIGURE 3.5). Although this is true for both traditional and deep sidecut skis, it is more difficult to accomplish on traditional skis, especially at slow speeds.

Start a carved turn in a narrow wedge. At the top of a turn, shift your weight onto the inside edge of the outside ski. In the wedge position, the outside leg is at an angle to the upper body. As a result, the ski is already tipped on edge. Be patient; do not twist your foot/ski. As the edge of the weighted ski "bites" into the snow, a circular arc will develop (see *Model the Ski*, Chapter 1).

FIGURE 3.6

Over-edge the outside ski to feel clearly the sensation of the ski slicing through the snow.

NOTE FOR DEEP SIDECUT SKIS. When a deep sidecut ski is tipped on edge, the design of the ski will make it easier to experience carving.

The wide tips of deep sidecut skis turn more sharply than the narrower tips of traditional skis. Therefore, separate the tips of your skis more than usual so that you will be less apt to cross your tips.

EDGE LOCKS. An edge lock is an exaggerated maneuver in which an extreme amount of edge angle is used (FIGURE 3.6). In this exercise, the ski is "locked" on a steep edge. It is an effective exercise to explore edging, the engagement of the edge on the snow.

From a *gliding* wedge, greatly increase the edge angle of one ski to move in the direction it tracks. Release the edge by decreasing the edge angle. Then, greatly increase the edge of the other ski to move in the direction it points.

NOTE FOR DEEP SIDECUT SKIS. A deep sidecut ski will scribe a noticeable arc when it is tipped on edge at an extreme angle.

VARY WEDGE WIDTH. The width of your stance greatly affects your speed of descent. A wide position places the skis onto steep edge angles which causes braking, or slowing to occur. A wide stance is used to control speed on steep terrain (FIGURE 3.7). In a narrow stance, the skis are comparatively flatter. With less edge engagement, speed increases (FIGURE 3.8).

A parallel stance can evolve from a narrow wedge when weight transfer to the outside ski is combined with an active *rotary* movement of the inside leg.

UPPER BODY EXERCISES. This exercise identifies unnecessary movement of the upper body (FIGURE 3.9). If you suspect a problem, use this visual exercise to assess and to help correct your

FIGURE 3.7 and FIGURE 3.8
Speed is slower in a wide wedge (top) than in a narrower wedge (bottom).

body position.

Loop one ski pole strap over the basket of the other pole. Then, place the ski poles around your hips and connect the other side. Make sure the poles are level. Ideally, the poles should remain perpendicular to the fall line as you ski rhythmic turns down the hill. Ski a series of wedge turns and notice if the poles tip or turn, indicating:

 (a) leaning the upper body toward the center of the turn—poles on hips tip instead of staying level
 (b) turning the upper body away from the fall line—poles on hips start the turn before the skis turn
 (c) leaning and turning the upper body—poles on hips tip and turn ❄

FIGURE 3.9

The ski poles should not tip or turn.

SKI POLE ACTION

POLE STRAPS. It is important to use grips with straps for an effective pole swing and pole plant. To use them properly, move your hand up through the loop of the strap, and then down, gripping the strap and pole. Adjust the straps so they fit snugly around your gloves with your hand positioned at the top of the grip (FIGURE 3.10).

FIGURE 3.10

Adjust the strap so that your hand is at the top of the grip.

ARM POSITION. Keep your arms in front of your body and your hands several inches wider than the width of your body. Hold your poles with a firm, yet not tense, grip (FIGURE 3.11). Point the ski pole tips behind you.

POLING ACROSS FLAT TERRAIN. Ski poles are initially used to propel yourself across flat terrain. Plant your poles on both

FIGURE 3.11
Arms should be in a relaxed position. Do not raise your shoulders.

sides of your skis at a point in front of the bindings. To slide forward, rock forward with your arms extended and then push down and back with your outstretched arms (FIGURE 3.12). ❄

FIGURE 3.12
*Push down and back
to propel forward.*

TURN SHAPE

DRAWING TURNS. Use your gloved finger to draw smooth, round arcs in the snow (FIGURE 3.13). Draw completed turns without straight lines connecting the turns. Turns should be *linked* so that the completion of one arc leads directly into the start of the next arc. Linked, round shaped turns help you to control your speed smoothly without having to jam on your edges and skid in order to slow down.

Some skiers incorrectly depict turns as zig-zag in shape. This misunderstanding is often reflected in their turns which tend to be quickly pivoted from one direction to the other.

HAND TURNS. While standing or sitting, visualize turns using hand movements to represent skis (FIGURE 3.14). While holding your hands next to each other, turn and tip your "skis" from edge to edge through round shaped turns. Emphasize the outside "ski" of the turn.

FIGURE 3.13

In linked turns, the path of the skis should always be curved, without straight paths connecting the curves.

STUDY ARCS. You can tell a clean, carved turn by looking at your tracks in the snow. Work toward a narrow rounded path in the snow and not a broad swath.

VARY TURN SIZE. A large, or *long radius*, turn requires a gradual tipping of the skis on edge in comparison to a small, or *short radius*, turn. As you ski, vary the size of your turns.

CONTROL SPEED. In a wedge, speed can be decreased by widening the wedge and/or by continuing to turn in an arc until the outside ski points across the hill before starting into the next turn. Speed can be increased by narrowing the wedge and/or by starting into the next turn *before* the outside ski points across the hill.

On steep terrain, it is necessary to finish the turn with skis pointing across the hill to control speed. At the moment of turn completion on flatter terrain, the skis should point diagonally down the hill, carrying more speed.

Link turns with very round and completed arcs and then compare them to turns that are completed diagonally on the hill.

LEAD FOLLOW. In a lead-follow formation, the leader determines the size, shape, and speed of the turns. The follower tries to stay in the leader's tracks (FIGURE 3.15). When a technically better skier is in the lead, the follower can focus on a specific movement to imitate, such as arm position. Or, specific movements can be predetermined for imitation by the follower. ❋

FIGURE 3.14 (top)
Use hand movements to illustrate
and understand ski movements.

FIGURE 3.15
Look at the leader's skis to follow
in the tracks.

TERRAIN AND SNOW CONDITIONS

GENTLE TERRAIN. Wedge turns should be primarily skied on gentle, "green" runs. The challenge for skiers of this ability is to learn basic skills and movement patterns. Difficult terrain provides an added variable that can lead to bad habits and be stressful.

STEEPER TERRAIN. In areas where the hill becomes steeper, the edge angle on the outside ski of the turn must increase in order for the ski to grip the snow and not slip sideways. As the edge angle increases, the skier's center of mass should move slightly toward the inside of the turn to balance. The upper body should remain vertical.

FIGURE 3.16

Your upper body follows a smooth path while your legs flex and extend to remain in contact with irregular terrain.

VARIABLE TERRAIN. Even on gentle slopes, the terrain can be variable. Washboard-like rolls, *side hills*, changes in pitch, and gentle bumps need to be negotiated in order to ski smoothly down the hill. Terrain features provide an opportunity to explore movement patterns that enhance balance. These experiences will pro-

vide the foundation for adapting to abrupt changes on difficult terrain in the future.

To maintain balance over undulations in terrain, such as rolls and bumps, keep your upper body stable and use leg action to ride smoothly over terrain changes (FIGURE 3.16). Your upper body should travel a smooth path while your legs flex and extend to remain in contact with the irregular terrain. Let the bump raise your legs underneath your upper body causing your joints to flex. Rock forward at the top of the bump to maintain balance while your skis descend quickly on the steep downward side of the bump. Extend your legs to keep your skis on the snow. Always, keep your hands in front of your body for balance.

On side hill terrain, or *fall-aways*, the slope falls away to one side as well as down the hill. To avoid skidding sideways it is important to be balanced on the outside ski of the turn and to edge your ski sufficiently in order to grip the snow (FIGURE 3.17).

FIGURE 3.17
When the slope falls away, make sure to stand on the inside of your foot on the outside ski to engage the edge sufficiently.

HARD SNOW AND ICE. On hard snow or ice, speed can increase quickly. To control speed, ski round-shaped turns and complete each turn with the outside ski pointing across the hill. Gradual tipping of the outside ski on its edge will develop a smooth arc. With abrupt edge movements, the ski will not grip the hard snow as well, resulting in chatter and sideways skidding.

POWDER SNOW. When you ski on a hard snow surface, it is primarily the edge of the ski that touches the snow. In powder conditions, however, skis often sink below the surface. When this happens, the entire base of the ski is supported by snow. The snow creates resistance as it is pushed away, causing the skier to descend at a slower speed. Dense, heavy snow (high moisture content) slows the skier to a greater degree than light powder (low moisture content).

It is very difficult to ski in a wedge position in deep, dense snow conditions. When one ski is weighted more than the other, it can sink and slow down, pulling the skier off-balance. If the snow is not too dense or deep, narrow your wedge, turn through a shallower arc, and/or ski slightly steeper terrain. Try small, shallow turns straight down the hill, transferring weight by pedaling from foot to foot. Weight the inside ski sufficiently so that it does not get pushed around by the snow.

CRUD SNOW. The expression, "crud snow" is often used to mean deep snow that has been cut up by ski tracks. This snow is inconsistent in depth and, therefore, difficult to ski. Balance is critical since skis accelerate abruptly as they enter areas where snow has been scraped away, and decelerate where it has been piled. Seek the balance point under your foot to regain balance over the center of your skis. ✳

LESSON PLAN

Select the exercises or subjects from each catagory that you would like to practice. Refer back to this outline to change your lesson plan for subsequent days.

WARM YOUR BODY. Refer to Chapter 9, *On the Snow Warm-up* for suggestions of exercises to warm and stretch your body.

RHYTHM AND REVIEW. Ski rhythmic turns in a wedge on smooth, gentle terrain. Consider one of the following themes to keep in mind as you ski:

(a) aim your upper body straight down the hill

(b) keep your hands in front of your body

(c) look ahead

(d) transfer your weight to the outside ski of the turn

(e) extend your legs to start the turn, flex to finish

(f) feel the edge of the ski cut through the snow in a circular arc

(g) control speed by completing a round arc

DIRECTED FREE SKIING. You may encounter different terrain features or snow conditions even on beginning, "green" terrain. Select one subject from the previous list to keep in mind as you negotiate the terrain. As you gain confidence, explore different size turns and vary your speed. Use verbal cues, such as "left, right" to focus attention on the outside ski, and "turn, turn" to help develop a rhythm. (See *Verbal Cues*, Chapter 10, *Perceptual Skills*.)

SCHOOLWORK. Select from the following exercises. Review the description and photographs earlier in this chapter that coincide with the exercises you choose (listed by title).

(a) *The Outside Ski*
(b) *Flex and Extend*
(c) *Edge Locks*
(d) *Upper Body Exercise*
(e) *Arm Position*
(f) *Poling Across Flat Terrain*
(g) *Study Arcs*
(h) *Follow the Leader* (Chapter 10, *Perceptual Skills*)

MOUNTAIN PLAYGROUND. Although you are limited to beginning terrain at this ability level, select a variety of runs to broaden your experiences. Explore different wedge widths. Then, work toward a narrow wedge. Review the following subjects to prepare for variable terrain and the following conditions:

(a) *Hard Snow and Ice*
(b) *Powder Snow*
(c) *Crud Snow*

SLOW AND EASY. Ski on gentle terrain. A narrow wedge is less tiresome than a wide wedge.

LESSON PLAN EXAMPLE:

WARM YOUR BODY.
(a) *Run in Place*
(b) *Knee Lift*
(c) *Head Movement*

(d) *Arm Routine*

(e) *Hip Circles*

(f) *Side Stretch*

(g) *Twisting Movements*

(h) *Calf Stretch*

(i) *Inside Leg Stretch*

RHYTHM AND REVIEW.

(a) keep your hands in front of your body

(b) aim your upper body straight down the hill

DIRECTED FREE SKIING.

(a) look ahead

(b) control speed by completing a round arc

SCHOOLWORK. Select from the following exercises. Review the description and photographs earlier in this chapter that coincide with the exercises you choose (listed by title).

(a) *Edge Locks*

(b) *Study Arcs*

MOUNTAIN PLAYGROUND. Explore beginning terrain.

SLOW AND EASY. Turn in a narrow wedge on gentle terrain. ❄

Arapahoe Basin, late June

CHAPTER 4:
PARALLEL TURNS

A parallel turn is the primary goal for most beginning skiers. A parallel stance allows you to ski faster and ski more varied terrain.

You are ready to progress to this chapter if you ski comfortably and competently in a narrow wedge. The following exercises and progressions will help you advance from beginning to intermediate terrain. This chapter is appropriate for parallel skiers at all levels of expertise since it introduces and develops necessary skills.

TURN DESCRIPTION. In a parallel stance, the tips and the tails of the skis are at an equal distance apart. The parallel relationship of the inside ski is more natural than the angled position of the inside ski in a wedge.

For a parallel turn, begin in a parallel turn stance with your feet apart for balance and stability. At the start of the turn, slowly extend your legs and transfer your weight to the outside ski of the turn. The extension flattens your skis on the snow so that you can

FIGURE 4.1

In a parallel turn, the inside ski is steered to coincide with the path of the outside ski.

tip onto opposite edges and turn down the hill more easily. Increase the edge angle on your outside ski. Steer your inside leg/ski to correspond with the path of the outside ski (FIGURE 4.1). When your upper body and skis face down the hill, lower your body by flexing your ankles, knees and torso through the remainder of the turn. Aim your upper body toward the mid-way point of the arc of the next turn. Time your pole swing to coincide with the extension of your legs. Touch your pole on the snow at the same time you begin to change edges for the upcoming turn. ✳

BALANCE ROUTINE ON ONE SKI. Sliding on one ski will challenge and improve your balance. When you have accomplished the following exercises, you should feel more comfortable exploring new movement patterns. For these exercises, you can either lift one ski off the snow, or remove it entirely. Note that at some ski areas, permission to ski on one ski must be obtained from the ski area management.

Slide down a gentle slope on one ski and then the other. Try

BALANCING EXERCISES

FIGURE 4.2

After you have accomplished each exercise separately, combine the exercises into routines. This example includes hopping, touching the snow and swinging the free leg.

FIGURE 4.3

Step back and forth over a pole to rehearse shifting weight from one ski to the other.

the following exercises as you balance on one ski. (FIGURE 4.2)

(a) rock forward, rock backward, find the centered position

(b) hop lifting the tip, tail or the whole ski

(c) reach for the sky, touch the snow

(d) swing the free leg forward and backward

(e) clap hands (without ski poles)

SIDE STEP OVER POLE. Side stepping is a balancing exercise that helps to develop the transfer of weight from one ski to the other (FIGURE 4.3).

Place one of your ski poles on the snow. Stand beside the pole. Then, step over the pole with the ski that is closest to the pole. Touch the ski on the snow momentarily before bringing it back to its original place. Cross this ski back and forth over the pole before repeating the exercise with the other ski. ❄

SKILL DEVELOPMENT

FIGURE 4.4

Try to move like a shadow as you copy your partner's steps.

SIDE STEP SHADOW CHASE. This exercise develops weight transfer and edging skills. Also, it is a good warm-up exercise to start the day or to get moving after a cold chairlift ride (FIGURE 4.4).

Face a partner on flat or gentle terrain. As the leader, take single or multiple steps sideways, changing your direction often. The follower attempts to copy your steps. Use the uphill edge of your downhill ski to provide a platform from which you can step up the hill. Step down the hill onto an edged ski so the ski does not slip. Move quickly from ski to ski.

TRAVERSE. A traverse provides the experience of gliding across the hill in a parallel ski relationship (FIGURE 4.5).

Travel across the hill, with both skis tipped onto their uphill edges. Keep more of your weight on your downhill ski. Each ski should track and not slip or skid sideways, losing the edge. Stand in a balanced, vertical position with the uphill ski and the uphill side of the body slightly ahead.

TRAVERSE EXERCISES. Practice traversing on the downhill ski while tapping the uphill ski lightly on the snow. Increase the length of time that you hold the uphill ski off the snow until you can traverse across the hill on one ski.

FIGURE 4.5

Leave "railroad tracks" in the snow.

FIGURE 4.6

While in a traverse, lift one ski, resume the traverse position, and then, touch your boots.

Try the following tasks separately, then link them together into a routine (FIGURE 4.6).

(a) reach for the sky, touch the snow

(b) touch your boot tops

(c) march from foot to foot, sliding on one foot between each step

(d) alternate sliding one ski forward as you pull the other foot back in a shuffling manner

(e) lift one ski completely off the snow

(f) jump on both skis

(g) hop on one ski

FIGURE 4.7

Traverse toward a target such as a ski pole.

TRAVERSE TARGET. Use a target to provide a reference point to ski toward in a traverse (FIGURE 4.7). Aim directly at the target as you begin your traverse. The sidecut of your skis will slightly curve your track in the uphill direction, above the target. If you fall below the target, look at your tracks to determine if your edges are slipping.

NOTE FOR DEEP SIDECUT SKIS. A deep sidecut ski that is set on edge will scribe a sharper arc up the hill.

SIDESLIP. The sideslip is a maneuver in which you slip sideways down the hill. It is an effective exercise to explore edging movements. Also, the sideslip provides a way to descend difficult ter-

FIGURE 4.8
Slip directly sideways, using your edges to control the speed of your descent.

rain (FIGURE 4.8).

Stand in a traverse position with your skis perpendicular to the slope and tipped on uphill edges. Turn your head to look down the hill. Extend to flatten your skis so that you can slip sideways down the hill. Flex slightly, moving your knees uphill, to edge sufficiently to control your speed of descent. To come to a stop, bend your legs and move your knees in the uphill direction to increase the edge angle on the snow surface.

Use this exercise to explore degrees of edging. The flatter your skis are on the surface of the snow, the faster you will descend. As the edge angle increases, speed will diminish or stop. The sideslip also provides an indicator for fore/aft balance. When balanced on the center of the ski, the skier should slip directly down the hill without forward or rearward motion.

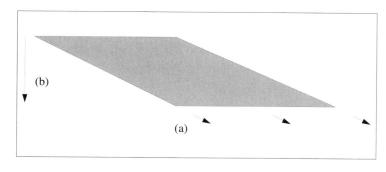

FIGURE 4.9

In this illustration of the path of the skis in a forward sideslip, the skis travel at a diagonal (a) to the fall line (b).

FORWARD SIDESLIP. From a moving traverse, extend to reduce the edge angle in order to slip sideways while traveling forward. A diagonal path down the hill will result (FIGURE 4.9). Explore the different paths between pure traverse and pure sideslip.

BOOT TURNS. If you start a turn in a wedge position, this exercise will help develop the simultaneous leg movements that are necessary for a parallel entry (FIGURE 4.10).

For this exercise, look for a hard snow surface on moderate terrain. With your skis off, stand in position to start a turn. Tip and turn both feet at the same time as you slide forward. If necessary, push with your poles to slide.

FIGURE 4.10

Without skis, practice the action of turning both feet, maintaining a parallel position throughout the turn.

PIVOT SLIP. The pivot slip promotes a parallel turn entry and develops strong rotary movements of both legs underneath a stable upper body at the start of the turn (FIGURE 4.11).

FIGURE 4.11

Plant the pole as a pivot point for this maneuver.

Stand in a traverse position on a moderate slope. Turn your upper body to face down the hill and plant your downhill pole in the fall line. Flatten your skis on the snow while moving your body down the hill. This will make it easier to pivot your skis into a sideslip facing the opposite direction. Pivot around your ski pole, ending the pivot downhill from the point where the pole was planted. Finish in a lower stance to increase the edge angle and control the sideslip. Link pivot slips in both directions.

On gentle terrain, evolve the pivot slip into round-shaped turns by slowing the pivoting action and increasing the edge angle.

SAFETY STOP. A *safety stop* is an essential maneuver to learn to stop quickly or avoid obstacles (FIGURE 4.12).

Start from a tall stance, sliding straight down a smooth slope. Quickly drop to a lower position as you pivot your skis to a sideslip position. The rapid downward body movement momentarily lightens your skis so they are easier to pivot. Turn your legs only, keeping your upper body facing down the hill throughout the maneuver. Increase the edge angle of your skis to slow down and come to a stop.

Develop this maneuver into the finish of a rounded turn by

FIGURE 4.12
Use the safety stop when you need to stop quickly.

slowing the pivoting action and increasing the edge angle.

FIGURE 4.13

Begin each garland turn in a
wedge and finish in a parallel
stance to become comfortable with
the movement pattern. Then,
progress to a parallel position
throughout the entire maneuver.

GARLAND TURNS. *Garland* turns provide an alternative to skiing straight down the fall line. They are helpful for descending difficult terrain.

To start a garland, direct your skis across the hill. Turn down the hill, and then away from the fall line in your original direction of travel (FIGURE 4.13). Link garland turns in a rhythmic pattern to

descend diagonally. When you reach the side of the slope, make a full turn to head in the opposite direction.

Garland turns promote repetitive practice of the first half or the second half of a turn. Use the beginning of a garland turn to practice steering your skis down the hill, into the fall line. Emphasize the transfer of weight to the outside ski of the turn as you steer both skis (turn and tip simultaneously) toward the fall line. Use the completion of a garland turn to develop better edge control and minimize skidding. As you turn away from the fall line, balance on the new outside ski and flex your legs to increase edging.

LIFT THE INSIDE SKI. To improve balance on the outside ski of a turn, lift your inside ski off the snow (FIGURE 4.14). If the tip of the ski is higher than the tail, try lifting the tail only to move your weight forward, over the balance point (FIGURE 4.15). Experiment with lifting your inside ski high, and then just high enough to clear the snow. Afterwards, place your inside ski on the snow so that it feels as light as a feather on the snow as your outside ski controls the arc of your turns (FIGURE 4.16).

CRAYON MARK. Pretend you have a crayon under the inside edge of your foot (the wrapper has been peeled off the crayon). Pretend, too, that your feet, instead of your skis, are scribing turns on the snow. When you carve a turn, the crayon leaves a thin colored mark in the snow. When your feet (skis) skid, the mark is much wider—a sideways rubbing of the crayon. Strive for thin *curvilinear* marks left in the snow.

The inside foot should leave a parallel mark that is wider and a lighter shade of color. The mark is wider and lighter because the inside foot is not weighted enough to bend the ski into an arc that matches or exceeds the arc of the uphill ski. Thus it marks a broader swath on the snow as it moves parallel to the outside ski.

LEAPING. It is difficult to complete a turn successfully if you are off-balance at the beginning of the turn. A jumping, or leaping

FIGURE 4.14 (top), FIGURE 4.15 (middle), FIGURE 4.16 (bottom)
Lift the inside ski off the snow (top) to balance on the outside ski. Lift the tail (middle) to discourage leaning back. Place the ski lightly on the snow (bottom).

FIGURE 4.17

Leap to start your turn.

action encourages a balanced position. Also, this motion encourages leg extension, and helps to develop a parallel ski relationship at the start of a turn (FIGURE 4.17).

First, jump in ski boots without skis. Bend your ankles, knees, and torso, and then spring upward. Try jumping as high as you can. Then, jump only high enough to clear the snow. Next, add your skis and jump from a standstill. If your weight is too far forward, it is difficult to jump and only your ski tails will come off the snow. If your weight is too far back, you can raise your ski tips only. Jump from a centered stance to lift your skis entirely off the snow.

In a turn, balance over the center of your skis and then spring upward. Plant your pole to push off as you leap. Turn your skis slightly in the air and land on your edges.

Leaping is an exaggerated form of body extension. Replace this movement with a smooth, gradual extension of your legs to begin a turn. The extension flattens your skis on the snow, making them easier to steer. As you extend, feel the inside edge of your outside ski in order to control the arc of your turns.

BOBBING. Your skis tend to skid sideways when your legs are stiff. Bobbing develops flexing movements of the legs which absorb the excess pressure that can build on your skis through the completion of a turn. Flexing the legs on an inclined slope also increases the edge angle, continuing the turn (FIGURE 4.18).

Practice bending your ankles and knees by bobbing up and down. Slowly extend to begin each turn. When your skis point down the hill, start bobbing. Continue the bobbing action until your turn is completed. Experiment moving slowly and smoothly in comparison to bobbing quickly. As you flex, balance on the inside edge of your outside ski in order to control the arc of your turns.

Instead of multiple bobs during the turn completion, slowly bob so that one downward motion occurs during the second half of the turn. By extending your knees and ankles to begin a turn, and flexing to complete the turn, you can develop smooth, round shaped arcs.

FIGURE 4.19

To skate, push off an angled, edged ski and glide onto the other ski.

SKATING. Skating promotes the transfer of weight from one ski to the other, and the development of a secure edge (FIGURE 4.19).

Practice skating on flat terrain. Push off an angled, edged ski and glide onto the other ski. After pushing with one ski, bring it parallel to the other ski before the next skating step. Repetitive skating with the same foot pushing off makes skating easier to learn. Remember to bring your skis together to glide between skating push-offs. ✳

SKI POLE ACTION

POLE SWING. From a balanced stance, practice pole swing using wrist movement primarily. Touch the tip of your pole lightly in the snow. Only minimal arm movements are necessary to swing the pole (FIGURE 4.20).

Then, practice your pole swing while sliding straight down a gentle hill. Touch your pole in the snow and then tip your hand downward to keep your hand in front of your body while pivoting the pole off the snow.

TOUCH/PLANT. A pole can be touched lightly or planted hard in the snow. A light pole touch promotes the timing and rhythm of turns. Pole contact that is too hard can disrupt the flow of movement from one turn to the next. But in situations such as skiing through bumps, a hard, or very deliberate pole plant is helpful for stabilizing the upper body.

TIMING OF THE POLE ACTION. At first, touch your pole in the snow and turn around your pole. With practice, the pole swing occurs simultaneously with the extension of your body at the start of a turn. The pole touches the snow at the moment of edge change (FIGURE 4.21).

FIGURE 4.20

To plant your pole, think about swinging the tip forward rather than moving your whole arm.

INCORRECT ARM MOVEMENT. Unnecessary arm movements can disturb balance and make it difficult to use ski poles effectively. Often, underlying problems can be identified when skiers try to optimize their arm positions. Examples of incorrect arm positions and the possible consequences of these positions follow.

(a) Arms that are held too high lessen stability and cause weight to move behind the balance point.

(b) Arms that are held too low encourage a forward bend at the waist.

(c) Arms that are back cause weight to move back.

(d) Arm separation that is too narrow inhibits lateral angulation and a countered position.

(e) Arms that are spread too wide inhibit pole swing and cause body rotation.

(f) An outside arm that is too high causes leaning *(banking)* toward the center of the turn.

(g) An inside arm that is too low also causes leaning (banking) toward the center of the turn.

(h) Arms that cross in front of the body cause rotation of the upper body, which can cause skidding. ✳

FIGURE 4.21
Touch your pole lightly in the snow as you change edges.

FOOT ARCS. Pushing the ski away from the body to attain an edge is a common error (FIGURE 4.22). In order to develop an arc, the outside ski must be weighted, edged and turned. In this way, the ski travels forward through the arc of the turn. Sideways skidding is minimized, leaving clear arcs in the snow (FIGURE 4.23).

An exercise to illustrate the difference between these actions is illustrated in the accompanying photographs. Without skis, first push your foot sideways, increasing the edge angle. Then, scribe arcs by simultaneously turning and edging your foot. Notice how the foot travels forward through the arc of this turn.

TURN SHAPE

FIGURE 4.22
Pushing the foot sideways causes the skis to skid in a turn (left).

FIGURE 4.23
In a carved turn, the foot travels forward in an arc (right).

FIGURE 4.24

Notice the spray of snow from the skis in a skidded turn (left).

FIGURE 4.25

Notice the bend of the ski in a carved turn (right).

SKIDDING/CARVING. Compare skidded, zig-zag shaped turns with round and completed carved turns. In skidded turns, the ski slides forward and sideways down the hill (FIGURE 4.24). In carved turns, the ski travels forward through the arc of the turn and the tails of the skis follow the line of the tips (FIGURE 4.25).

VARY SIZE. Explore small, medium and large sized turns. Practice maintaining a consistent turn size, rhythm and speed, and also practice changing the turn size, rhythm and speed.

CONTROL SPEED. Ski round shaped turns on steep terrain, completing each turn with skis pointing across the hill, perpendicular to the fall line. Use completed turns to control speed instead of pivoting skis sideways and skidding. ❄

TERRAIN and SNOW CONDITIONS

EASIEST TERRAIN. Learning new skills should take place on easiest, "green" runs. Look for groomed runs in order to concentrate on the maneuver without the distraction of inconsistent surface conditions.

MORE DIFFICULT TERRAIN. As your ability improves, more difficult, "blue" terrain can be explored. If the challenge of the terrain inhibits performance or progress, return to easier terrain.

SMALL BUMPS. Turning on small bumps can help develop the *rotary action* of both legs and improve the parallel turn entry. In a field of bumps, the uphill part (top) of each bump provides the flattest terrain. The downhill part of each bump slants steeply downward. Control your speed by turning sharply on the top of the bump (FIGURE 4.26). Plant your pole straight down the hill for stability and to direct your upper body down the hill (FIGURE 4.27). Rock forward and turn both skis at the same time. Your forward commitment will allow you to stay balanced over your skis as they quickly descend the steep downslope of the bump. Press your ski tips down to maintain contact with the surface of the snow. Although both skis are turned simultaneously, weight and edge the downhill ski sufficiently to hold on the steep downhill side of the bump.

A common problem that occurs at this level is caused by keeping the planted pole in the snow too long. When this happens, the

FIGURE 4.26
Turn sharply on the flat, uphill side of the bump to control your speed

FIGURE 4.27

The upper body aims straight down
the hill as the pole is planted.

inside hand gets left behind, twisting the skier's upper body away from the direction of travel (down the hill). It also causes the skier to lean uphill making it difficult to start into the next turn. To avoid this, tip your hand downward following the pole plant in order to keep your hand in front of your body and stay in balance.

LONG TURNS IN BUMPS. Skiing medium to long radius turns in small bumps improves balance and leg movement. Try to maintain ski/snow contact, to keep the arc round, to absorb with your legs, and to keep your upper body quiet.

TERRAIN GARDEN. Many ski areas have terrain gardens with features such as rolls, bumps, pedal bumps, drop-offs, compressions, ridges, banked turns and jumps. These terrain features prepare you for natural challenges that you may confront while skiing on the mountain. Man-made terrain gardens are usually found on gentle slopes, so they provide excellent conditions for practice. The balance exercises below will be difficult for the beginning skier, but they should be mastered over a period of time to progress to expert skiing ability.

Refer to *Variable Terrain* in Chapter 3, to review skiing over rolls and bumps. Pedal bumps consist of two rows of bumps over which one foot is on top of a bump while the other foot is down in a *trough*. These features in a terrain garden may be very uneven and abrupt. Attempt to keep your upper body traveling along a smooth path down the hill, while your legs flex and extend to absorb pressure and remain in contact with the snow.

A drop-off is a region where the slope drops away at a steep angle. It is important to anticipate this change in pitch by rocking forward. In this way, your upper body will move down the hill and not be left back as your skis accelerate down the steep slope. After you enter the steep slope, focus on staying balanced over the center of your skis.

A compression zone is the transition curve between a very steep slope and much flatter terrain. When you enter the transition, your skis tend to slow down abruptly causing a concentration of upward and rearward force on your body. It is important to enter a compression in a fairly tall stance so you can absorb the force by flexing your joints. Enter the compression with your weight slightly back since the abrupt change of speed will tend to lurch your body forward.

A ridge is a narrow path where both sides of the ridge fall away steeply. To ski along a ridge, turn on the sides of the ridge. The transition between turns (completion of one turn and start of the next turn) occurs at the top of the ridge. Turning on the side of a ridge is the same as turning on a side hill. Since the sides of a ridge can be very steep, it is necessary to weight and edge the outside ski of the turn in order to grip the snow. Change edges at the top of the ridge in preparation for the new turn. Rock forward to stay balanced while descending on the other side; extend your legs to keep your skis on the snow.

Skiing a banked turn feels very different from skiing on a side hill. Instead of the hill falling away to the side, it raises upwards and supports your skis. You can lean or bank toward the center of the turn since less edge is necessary to grip the snow. With skis flatter on the snow surface, your weight can be more evenly distributed between both skis, although the outside ski should still control the arc of the turn. Focus on guiding both skis through the turn.

TERRAIN FEATURES. Practice newly acquired skills on rolling terrain, side hills and knolls. Balance is a critical issue when the pitch of the slope changes. Your proximity to the balance point on the sole of your foot will help you evaluate fore/aft balance.

HARD SNOW AND ICE. Smooth, round-shaped arcs are appropriate for hard snow and ice conditions (see *Hard Snow and Ice*, Chapter 3). Slightly widen your stance on ice in case your edges do not hold. In a wider stance, your ski will slip sideways until the edge angle is sufficient to grip the snow. If you start in a narrow stance, the ski has much farther to slip before the edge engages. By then, the ski's momentum will usually cause the slipping to continue regardless of the edge angle.

DEEP SNOW. When a few inches of snow has fallen on top of a solid base, weighting the outside ski to control the arc of the turn is still effective. But as snow deepens, the skier's weight should be more equally distributed. If one ski is weighted more than the other, it will sink and slow down, pulling the skier off-balance. A narrow stance helps to keep weight distributed on both skis. Although both skis are turned at the same time, the skier's legs should remain independent in their ability to flex and extend for balancing purposes.

The first turns are usually the hardest. Aim straight down the hill to gain enough speed in order to begin turning. Focus on rotary action of the lower body, turning both ski tips from side-to-side. Start with shallow arcs in the fall line, and then round out the turns as speed increases. Establish a rhythm to enhance movement from one turn to the next (FIGURE 4.28).

Skis are difficult to turn below the surface of the snow. In deep snow, it is easier to turn when the skis are close to the surface, on top of the snow, or in the air. Skiers can use flexion and extension movements to jump their skis out of the snow. Review *Leaping* under *Skill Development* in this chapter.

At the completion of a turn in soft snow, the ski can bend in a deeper arc than usual. When the skier extends in the direction of the next turn, the pressure that bends the ski is released at the moment the skier slows or stops his/her extension. This causes the ski to *rebound*, or spring back, propelling the skier out of the snow. The skier then turns and tips his/her skis before sinking into the snow for the next turn. ❄

FIGURE 4.28
You cannot hold back in deep snow. Stay close to the fall line to maintain sufficient speed. Set a rhythm and stay committed to your movement pattern.

LESSON PLAN

Select the exercises or subjects from each category that you would like to practice. Refer back to this outline to change your lesson plan for subsequent days.

WARM YOUR BODY. Refer to Chapter 9, *On the Snow Warm-up* for suggestions of exercises to warm and stretch your body.

RHYTHM AND REVIEW. Ski a series of rhythmic, medium sized turns at a slow speed on smooth, gentle terrain. Stay focused on a subject that you select from the following list.

    (a) a parallel stance with feet apart
    (b) a balanced stance, standing over the balance point
    (c) tipping and turning both feet/skis at the same time
    (d) weight transfer to the outside ski
    (e) weight along the inside edge of the outside foot
    (f) direction of the upper body
    (g) pole swing and touch
    (h) smooth movements
    (i) clean arcs in the snow (*Crayon Mark*)

DIRECTED FREE SKIING. Ski parallel turns on varying terrain. Select one subject from the previous list to keep in mind as you adapt your turns to different terrain, turn sizes and speeds. Also, listen to the sound of your skis on hard snow. The more your turns are skidded, the louder the sound will be. (See *Listen to Ski Sounds*, Chapter 10, *Perceptual Skills*.)

SCHOOLWORK. Select from the following exercises. Review the description and photographs earlier in this chapter that coincide with the exercises you choose.

    (a) *Traverse*
    (b) *Traverse Exercises*
    (c) *Sideslip*
    (d) *Forward Sideslip*
    (e) *Boot Turns*
    (f) *Pivot Slip*
    (g) *Safety Stop*
    (h) *Garland Turns*
    (i) *Lift the Inside Ski*
    (j) *Leaping*
    (k) *Bobbing*
    (l) *Skating*
    (m) *Skidding/Carving*
    (n) *Judging Speed* Chapter 10, *Perceptual Skills*)

MOUNTAIN PLAYGROUND. Select a variety of intermediate runs with different terrain features that you would like to ski. Be prepared to alter your plans to look for more difficult *or* less challenging terrain and snow conditions depending on the conditions of the day.

Ski round, completed turns on steep terrain to control your speed. Look for small bumps and terrain gardens to play in. Refer to *Hard Snow and Ice* and *Deep Snow* earlier in this chapter to prepare for these conditions.

SLOW AND EASY. Return to slow speed turns on gentle terrain.

LESSON PLAN EXAMPLE:

WARM YOUR BODY
   (a) *Knee Lift*
   (b) *Side Step Over Pole*
   (c) *Arm Circles*
   (d) *Hip Circles*
   (e) *Side Stretch*
   (f) *Inside Leg Stretch*
   (g) *Tail Stretch*

RHYTHM AND REVIEW
   (a) weight transfer to the outside ski
   (b) weight along the inside edge of the outside foot

DIRECTED FREE SKIING
   (a) *Crayon Mark*
   (b) smooth movements

SCHOOLWORK
   (a) *Traverse*
   (b) *Lift the Inside Ski*
   (c) *Skidding/Carving*

MOUNTAIN PLAYGROUND. Ski on runs that have small bumps.

SLOW AND EASY. "Cruise" on gentle terrain. ❈

Sensations, exhilaration

CHAPTER 5:
DYNAMIC SKIING

The skills that are introduced in *Parallel Turns* are refined in this chapter to develop dynamic carved turns. In skiing, "dynamic" refers to the rapid adjustments of body position that the skier makes to stay in balance. Emphasis is placed on medium and long radius turns in this chapter. "Medium radius" and "long radius" refer to the size of the turn measured by the distance from the center of the turn to the arc (path of the skis). These turns are characteristic of Giant Slalom turns.

Before reading this chapter, it is beneficial to review *A Curved Path*, Chapter 1.

FIGURE 5.1

In dynamic parallel turns, the inside edge of the outside ski plays a dominant role in controlling the arc of the turn.

TURN DESCRIPTION. In dynamic medium and long radius turns, there is a more active commitment of the body into the turn with more deliberate edge usage and more accurate guiding of the skis throughout the turn. Turns are characterized by a strong flow

of energy from one turn to the next. The intensity, duration and timing of the movements determine the size, shape and speed of the turn (FIGURE 5.1). ✳

L **IFT A SKI.** Practice turning in both directions on one ski with the other ski raised in the air (FIGURE 5.2). Turning with the inside ski off the snow is described in the previous chapter, under *Lift the Inside Ski.* Turning on the inside ski with the outside ski raised is more difficult. To accomplish this, begin on gentle terrain where your ski is fairly flat and, therefore, easier to turn on the snow surface. Plant your downhill pole firmly for support and pivot your inside (weighted) ski down the hill to start the turn. Lean to the inside of the turn and tip your inside ski on edge to control the arc of the turn. From this banked position, a deliberate pole plant down the hill will help you to move into the next turn. With practice, the pivoting action can be replaced with steering, a simultaneous turning *and* tipping of the ski onto the edge earlier in the turn.

BALANCING EXERCISES

FIGURE 5.2

Link turns on one ski to develop edging skills and balance.

ROYAL. Take turning on the inside ski one step further by lifting the raised ski into a royal position (FIGURE 5.3). To start a turn, step with the downhill leg diagonally down the hill onto the outside edge. Turn as described in *Lift a Ski*. Lift the outside ski behind and to the side of the inside ski. Turn the ski so that the tip points to the outside of the turn. At the finish of the turn, bring your outside ski down and parallel to your inside ski. Then, angle this ski and step onto it to perform a royal in the other direction.

FIGURE 5.3

A royal is a fun maneuver that challenges balance and the ability to use the outside edge of the ski.

SKI ON ONE SKI. Practice medium radius turns on one ski with the other ski removed. Start on gentle terrain and progress to more demanding terrain. At some ski areas, permission to ski on one ski must be obtained from the ski area management.

NO POLES. Sometimes skiers drag their ski poles in the snow to compensate for an unbalanced stance. The lack of balance may be due to leaning uphill, turning with the upper body, or having too much weight on the tails of the skis. Skiing with one pole or without poles is a good test for balance.

FIGURE 5.4

Keep your upper body quiet and hold your hands in front for balance as you ski without poles.

To ski without poles, keep your upper body quiet and hold your arms in front of your body for balance (FIGURE 5.4). As you ski, focus on the balance point along the inside edge of your outside foot. This will enable you to regulate fore/aft balance and to stay balanced over your outside ski.

As your skills develop, return to this exercise regularly in order to evaluate your stance and to become aware of unnecessary upper body movements that compensate for weak lower body activity. ❄

FORE/AFT BALANCE. In a static position, find the balance point over the mid-sole of your foot (over the ball of the foot for deep sidecut skis). From this point, rock forward to feel your weight move toward the front of your foot (ski tip). Rock backward to feel your weight move toward the back of your foot (ski tail). Then move only as little as necessary to feel your weight move toward the tip and then back toward the tail. Feel how very subtle body movements can change the distribution of weight. In general, only very small body movements are necessary to make fore/aft adjustments while skiing.

In turns, use subtle movements to work from your balance point. Adjust your weight forward to start the turn, in the center through the turn, and slightly back for the turn completion. This action moves the concentration of pressure against the snow from the front to the back of the skis. It helps the skis travel forward through the arc of the turn without braking sideways.

NOTE FOR DEEP SIDECUT SKIS. With a deep sidecut ski, the hourglass shape causes the flared tip and tail to cut into the snow when the ski is tilted on edge (refer to the model in *A Curved Path*). As a result, it is not necessary to pressure the tip and tail heavily. The ski will continue in the intended arc without fore and aft movement or with minimal movement.

ANGULATED POSITION. Angulation allows you to stay in balance on an edged ski by creating lateral angles in the body (FIGURE 5.5). In an angulated position, the center of mass of the body shifts toward the center of a turn, thereby compensating for the unbalancing effect of centrifugal force. Angulation can occur at the knees and hips (in combination with flexing of these joints) and in the spinal column (FIGURE 5.6 and FIGURE 5.7). In an angulated position, the upper body stays relatively vertical, with shoulders level, while the lower body (hip angulation) or the lower legs (knee angulation) are at a slant to the snow. Knee angulation is primarily used at slow speeds. A hip-angulated position is a stronger position because it depends on skeletal alignment from the foot to the hip for support. Hip angulation is used in higher speed turns and

SKILL DEVELOPMENT

FIGURE 5.5
Hip angulation occurs primarily at higher speeds and on steeper terrain.

FIGURE 5.6 (left)
*Knee angulation occurs
primarily at slower speeds
and on flatter terrain.*

FIGURE 5.7 (right)
Hip angulation.

on steeper terrain. Usually, subtle knee-angulating movements are used to make minor adjustments in edging in hip-angulated turns.

To work on hip angulation, develop body angles by practicing either high speed, carved wedge turns on gentle terrain, or slower wedge turns on steeper terrain. Continue to focus on an angulated position when you return to a parallel stance.

WEDGE/PARALLEL. In this exercise the relationship between wedge and parallel turn positions becomes very clear (FIGURE 5.8). The leader skis in a narrow wedge position while the follower skis

FIGURE 5.8
*The follower (in a parallel position)
imitates the angulated position of
the leader (in a wedge position).*

in a parallel position. The outside ski of the follower is placed in the track of the leader's outside ski. The follower (parallel skier) can observe the smooth arc of the turn, the action of the outside ski, and the body angles that are developed by the leader (wedge skier). The follower is forced to ski slowly, and therefore, he/she can concentrate on feeling the action of the outside ski.

BANKING. Banking means leaning inward, inclining toward the inside of the turn with a relatively straight body position (FIGURE 5.9). This action usually weights the inside ski of the turn, and reduces the pressure on the outside ski. With less weight on the outside ski, it is difficult to keep it bent in an arc through the turn. Sideways slipping often results.

With angulation, more body weight is applied to the outside ski. Ski a series of banked turns followed by a series of angulated turns. Feel the difference between leaning inward with the entire body (banking), and leaning only with the lower body while keeping the upper body vertical (angulation). You will enjoy the advantages of an angulated body position.

FIGURE 5.9
In a banked turn, the entire body inclines toward the center of the turn.

FIGURE 5.10

The outside hip is back in a countered position.

COUNTERED POSITION. In a traverse, a countered position means the uphill hip is slightly forward in relation to the downhill hip. In a turn, the inside hip is slightly forward in relation to the outside hip (FIGURE 5.10). Countering movements generally occur together with lateral angulation of the hip and spine. Together, a countered and hip-angulated stance inhibits the tails of the skis from skidding through the turn completion, and directs the upper body toward the upcoming turn.

A common mistake occurs when the upper body starts into a turn ahead of the lower body. This advances the outside hip ahead of the inside one, and causes the tails of the skis to skid.

The *Advanced Traverse Exercises* that follow are helpful for practicing a countered position while in a traverse. The *Javelin Turns* that follow encourage a countered position while in a turn.

FIGURE 5.11 (left)

In a traverse, flex and extend your downhill leg.

FIGURE 5.12 (right)

Flex and extend your uphill leg.

ADVANCED TRAVERSE EXERCISES. The following traverse exercises improve balance and edge control.

(a) Traverse across a steep slope. Increase your angulation and stand in a countered position in order not to "lose" the edge grip and slip sideways.

(b) On smooth terrain, step sideways to move your traverse line up the hill or down the hill.

(c) Lift your uphill ski. Flex and extend the downhill leg while traveling across the hill (Figure 5.11).

(d) Lift your downhill ski. Flex and extend the uphill leg (Figure 5.12).

(e) Traverse across medium sized bumps with your skis edged to maintain your line across the hill. Keep your upper body relatively still and absorb the terrain by bending and extending your legs. Let the bump bend your legs under your upper body as your skis climb up the bump. Then, rock forward and press your ski tips down the back, steep side of the bump to keep your skis on the snow.

JAVELIN TURNS. This exercise emphasizes a countered position with hip angulation (FIGURE 5.13). In a *javelin*, the skier balances on the outside ski of the turn with the inside ski lifted across the front of the outside ski. The placement of the inside ski makes it very difficult to rotate the outside hip through the turn. In linked

FIGURE 5.13
The position of the inside ski in a javelin turn encourages a countered and angulated body position.

javelin turns, the inside ski is returned to the snow, the weight is transferred and the next inside ski is raised and rotated as the turn is initiated.

Alternate, and repeat the following exercises to transfer the hip-angulated and countered position of a javelin turn to a parallel turn.

(a) six linked javelin turns, followed by

(b) six turns lifting the inside ski parallel, followed by

(c) six parallel turns placing the inside ski lightly on the snow

Also, try javelin turns without your ski poles (FIGURE 5.14). This requires a very accurate and balanced position.

FIGURE 5.14
A javelin turn without ski poles.

UPPER BODY DIRECTION. Finish turns long radius turns in a slightly countered position (the uphill side of the body and uphill ski are slightly ahead) and aim your upper body toward the mid-way point of the next turn. In shallower turns, your upper body will aim more down the hill in comparison to larger changes of direction. Focus on completing each turn in position for the next turn (FIGURE 5.15).

It is important that body extension movements carry the skier down the hill, and not vertically upward. Extend with your upper body facing in the direction of the mid-way point of the upcoming arc.

FIGURE 5.15
The skis continue to turn under the body to finish the turn as the upper body aims toward the upcoming turn.

FLOATERS. This exercise promotes early weight transfer and leg extension on the outside ski at the beginning of a turn (FIGURE 5.16). After completing a turn, transfer your weight to the uphill ski. Slowly rise as you traverse on this ski. Practice a smooth body extension, moving your body forward with the ski to "float" across the hill. Then tip this ski onto the inside edge, steering it into the next turn.

To develop *Floaters* into linked turns (without traverses), steer the tip of the uphill ski down the hill at the same time as you extend with your upper body facing down the hill.

FIGURE 5.16

In a floater, weight is transferred early in the turn to the new outside ski.

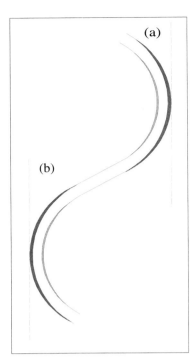

FIGURE 5.17

Ski a smooth transition from one fall line (a) to the next (b).

NOTE FOR DEEP SIDECUT SKIS. Floaters clearly define the early weight transfer that is necessary for carving on a deep sidecut ski.

FLOW. Focus on skiing from fall line to fall line to promote a continuous flow of movement through the transition phase between turns (FIGURE 5.17).

SPEED. Ski racers must be versatile to adjust to any situation in order to maximize every opportunity to increase speed. They have to adapt to the demands of constantly changing terrain and snow conditions as well as a dictated course of descent (race course). The intensity, duration, and timing of their movements determine the size, shape, and speed of their turns. The following chart shows how the interplay of *balance*, *rotary*, *edging*, and *pressure control* skills can maintain, decrease, or increase speed of travel. The same factors apply for recreational skiers, too.

SMOOTH PATH. The transition between turns allows a skier to move smoothly from one turn to the next. There are two types of transitions, as illustrated (FIGURE 5.18). In both cases, the center of mass of the body moves along a continuous curvilinear path. The center of mass never darts sideways into a discontinuous (zig-zag)

Factors	Decrease Speed	Maintain or Increase Speed
1. Turn Shape and Turn Completion	(a) sharper turn, shorter radius (b) arc interrupted by skidding (c) more completion	(a) shallower turn arc (b) carved arc (minimal skidding) (c) less completion
2. Edging	(a) skidded turn (b) more edge than necessary (c) hard edge at end of turn (d) staying on edge too long	(a) clean, carved turn (b) minimal edge angle (c) releasing the edge at end of turn
3. Weight Distribution	(a) weight too far forward, tails-skid (b) weight too far back, tips skid	(a) weight centered over balance point

path. In both cases, the legs and skis move from one side of the center of mass to the other. The *cross-over* transition is used between more distant or longer radius turns. In this case, the weighted skis are flattened after the first turn and then angled onto the opposite edges. Minimal steering is used, and the skier's weight holds the ski firmly on the snow. The diagram shows the smooth paths of the center of mass and the skis. The transition from edge to edge is relatively slow, although the skier's speed can be very high. The skier's legs are extended in both turns, but obviously they are angulated to opposite sides. The body crosses over the skis during the transition and professionals call this a *cross-over* transition.

The *cross-under* transition is used between tight, closely linked turns. As a result of rebound at the end of one turn, skis are unweighted abruptly. In this momentarily unweighted transition period, the skier quickly extends his/her legs toward the outside of the next turn to get on the opposite edges immediately. It is a dynamic, forceful action of the legs, while the center of mass of the body moves smoothly into the next turn. The legs quickly move laterally under the body, hence the name of the maneuver.

Before and after transition moves, it is always important to feel the inside edge of the outside foot/ski in order not to "lose" the edge grip and slip or skid sideways. ✳

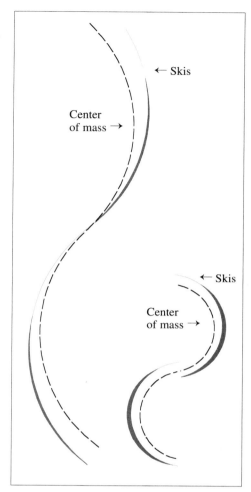

FIGURE 5.18
(a) Cross-over transition,
(b) Cross-under transition

SKI POLE ACTION

POLE ACTION. At the completion of a medium or long radius turn, the upper body faces toward the mid-way point of the upcoming arc. The swing of the ski pole aids in directing the upper body into the next turn. The pole touch occurs during the edge change. These movements assist a strong flow of energy that is characteristic of linked, carved turns.

NOTE FOR DEEP SIDECUT SKIS. On deep sidecut skis, the pole touch occurs with the leg extension after the skis have been tipped onto opposite edges.

INCORRECT POLE ACTION. Be aware of incorrect pole and arm action to help avoid problems. Excessive arm movements hinder balance. Following is a list of common faults:

(a) improper timing of pole plants (too early or too late)

(b) dropping the inside hand or lifting the outside hand

(c) hands positioned too high or too low

(d) planting out to the side

(e) crossing an arm in front of the body

(f) forward movement of the shoulder

(g) leaving the pole in the snow too long

(h) relying on dragging the poles for balance

(i) gripping the pole too tightly

TURN SHAPE

DIFFERENT TURN SHAPES. Edging, rotary, and pressure control skills can be blended in different ways to develop turns with different shapes for distinct purposes (FIGURE 5.19). A description of "C," "comma," and "J" shaped turns follows.

(a) Establish the edge early in the turn and ride the edge around, drawing a "C" shape in the snow. This turn is very round, smooth and versatile for most situations. The roundness of the turn makes it very effective for hard snow and icy conditions. Pressure builds gradually and is not intensified at any specific point in the turn. Because of this, the edges stay engaged throughout the turn and are less apt to skid. This turn provides the foundation and is a prerequisite for all other turns.

b) A "comma" shaped turn occurs when skis are redirected early in the turn. This requires a high edge angle and pressure very early in the turn. This turn is effective on very steep terrain where it is necessary to get the skis turned across the hill quickly to control speed. It minimizes the time spent in the fall line where speed can increase considerably.

The "comma" shaped turn is also characteristic of high speed turns that require a large change of direction, as can occur in race courses.

c) A "J" shaped turn occurs when the skis stay in the fall line longer and then rotary action is concentrated late in the turn. "J" turns are used in Slalom racing to maximize the time in the fall line (increasing speed) and minimize the time turning. The racer intensifies the rotary action into a small portion of the turn, getting on, and then off the edges quickly. Correct technique and precise timing make these turns effective.

The "J" turn is also effective in bump skiing where skiers accelerate in the troughs between bumps, and then control speed by turning sharply on the bumps.

A less accurate "J" shaped turn is typical for skiers who have not developed carving skills sufficiently to ski round shaped turns. Instead, rotary action happens with a quick pivot of the skis, and then the edges engage, resulting in skidded turns.

CONSISTENT RADIUS. On uneven terrain, practice skiing a consistent size turn. Look ahead to be prepared to absorb undulations in the terrain.

VARYING TURNS. On uneven terrain, vary the rhythm and radius of your turns to ski smoothly down the hill. On steeper pitches, complete your turns across the hill to control your speed. On flatter pitches, ski shallower arcs to carry speed. ※

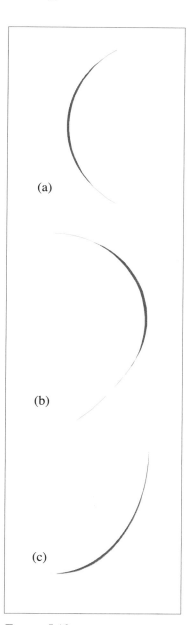

(a)

(b)

(c)

FIGURE 5.19

(a) "C" shape,

(b) "comma" shape,

(c) "J" shape turns

TERRAIN AND SNOW CONDITIONS

GENTLE TERRAIN. Remember to return to gentle terrain to try new movements and to learn difficult maneuvers. In this way, you can improve your technique comfortably and then, when you feel ready, apply your skill to more challenging terrain.

It is also helpful to ski on gentle terrain in order to assess your progress. Slower speeds require more accuracy and precision, and difficulties are often magnified at slow speeds.

MORE DIFFICULT TERRAIN. It is important to refine your skills and to perform consistently on "blue" terrain before you spend too much time on "black" terrain.

MOST DIFFICULT TERRAIN. Difficult terrain provides constant challenges for competent skiers (FIGURE 5.20). Miles of

FIGURE 5.20
The mountain, like a gigantic playground, provides you with endless movement possibilities and places to explore.

experience are necessary to adapt to demanding terrain and variable snow conditions.

ADVENTURE. Explore new terrain and different snow conditions (FIGURE 5.21). Terrain features and changeable snow conditions make every run a new experience. This creates a sense of adventure that contributes greatly to the excitement of skiing (see *Hard Snow and Ice* and *Deep Snow*, Chapter 4).

FIGURE 5.21

Spring snow conditions can be very inconsistent and challenging.

BUMP SKIING. Bump skiing is helpful for developing balance, quickness and reactions (see *Bump Skiing*, Chapter 6). Strive for a smooth flow of the upper body with only the legs moving up and down (FIGURE 5.22). ❋

LESSON PLAN

Select the exercises or subjects from each catagory that you would like to practice. Refer back to this outline to change your lesson plan for subsequent days.

WARM YOUR BODY. Refer to Chapter 9, *On the Snow Warm-up* for suggestions of exercises to warm and stretch your body.

RHYTHM AND REVIEW. Ski rhythmic, medium sized turns at a slow speed on smooth, gentle terrain. Stay focused on a subject that you select from the following list.

(a) standing on the inside edge of the outside ski

(b) standing over the balance point

(c) feet apart

(d) inside ski lead

(e) hands in front

FIGURE 5.22

Look ahead to ski smoothly in the bumps.

DIRECTED FREE SKIING. Ski parallel turns of different radii on intermediate, "blue" terrain. Select one subject from the previous list to keep in mind as you ski.

SCHOOLWORK. Select from the following exercises. Review the description and photographs earlier in this chapter that coincide with the titles you choose.

(a) *Lift a Ski*

(b) *Royal*

(c) *Ski on One Ski*

(d) *No Poles*

(e) *Fore/Aft Balance*

(f) *Angulated Position (practice high speed wedge turns)*

(g) *Wedge/Parallel*

(h) *Banking*

(i) *Countered Position*

(j) *Advanced Traverse Exercises*

(k) *Javelin Turns*

(l) *Upper Body Direction*

(m) *Floaters*

(n) *Flow*

(o) *Smooth Path*

(p) *Speed*

(q) *Pole Action*

(r) *Imagery* (*Perceptual Skills*, Chapter 10)

MOUNTAIN PLAYGROUND. Challenge yourself on the mountain. Look for variable and difficult terrain and snow conditions. Be prepared to alter your plans to look for more difficult *or* less challenging terrain and snow conditions depending on the conditions of the day.

Experiment with different turn shapes and sizes, and with a consistent radius over undulating terrain. Try long radius turns in the bumps.

SLOW AND EASY. Return to medium and long radius, round turns on gentle terrain.

LESSON PLAN EXAMPLE

WARM YOUR BODY.

(a) *Jumping Jacks*

(b) *Knee Lifts*

(c) *Downhill Racer*

(d) *Head Movement*

(e) *Arm Routine*

(f) *Side Stretch*

(g) *Twisting Movements*

(h) *Calf Stretch*

(i) *Inside Leg Stretch*

(j) *Tail Stretch*

(k) *Tip Stretch*

RHYTHM AND REVIEW.

(a) standing on the inside edge of the outside ski

DIRECTED FREE SKIING.

(a) feet apart

(b) inside ski lead

SCHOOLWORK.

(a) *Lift a Ski*

(b) *Angulated Position* (practice high speed wedge turns)

(c) *Javelin Turns*

MOUNTAIN PLAYGROUND. Ski medium and long radius turns in a variety of challenging terrain. Select runs that are wide enough to ski big turns without coming too close to the edge of the trail. Turn far enough across the hill to control the speed of fast descents.

SLOW AND EASY. Medium and long radius, round turns on gentle terrain. ❋

Challenging balance

CHAPTER 6:
QUICK TURNS

This chapter is filled with innovative and fun exercises to perfect quick turns. You will sharpen your skills and develop well-rounded abilities that will help you ski more diverse and challenging terrain.

Dynamic medium and long radius parallel turns provide the foundation for dynamic short radius turns. "Short radius" refers to the size of the turn measured by the distance from the center of the turn to the arc (path of the skis). The short radius turns described in this chapter are characteristic of Slalom turns.

TURN DESCRIPTION. In short radius turns, weight is transferred onto the outside ski. This is followed by a strong turning of both skis as they are tipped on edge. The rhythm and pace of movements is quicker than in longer radius turns. The skier faces down the hill since there is not time for the upper body to follow the direction of the skis. The pole plant is used for blocking upper body rotation as well as for timing. In turns with a deliberate edge set, the pole plant and edge set occur at the same time. In gliding turns, the pole touch occurs a moment later, with the extension at the beginning of the next turn. (FIGURE 6.1)

NOTE FOR DEEP SIDECUT SKIS. For a description of short radius turns on deep sidecut skis, turn to *Dynamic Carved Turns* and *Dynamic Short Radius Turns* in Chapter 8, *Deep Sidecut Carve.* ❋

BALANCING EXERCISES

SKI WITHOUT POLES. To improve your balance and the efficiency of your leg movements, ski without your ski poles (FIGURE 6.2).

As you ski, focus on the balance point along the inside edge of your outside foot in order to control the outside ski of the turn. In a rhythmic manner, transfer weight from outside foot (ski) to outside foot (ski). Aim your upper body down the hill. Maintain a quiet upper body with your arms held in front of your body for balance.

SKI "WITHOUT" BINDINGS. As you ski, pretend not to have bindings on your skis. Instead, you must depend on standing in a centered and balanced body position in order not to fall off your skis. This exercise is especially helpful for skiers who sit back or

FIGURE 6.1
Rhythmic short radius turns are consistent in turn size and speed.

hang forward against their boots.

SKI ON ONE SKI. As you link turns, lift one ski evenly off the snow (FIGURE 6.3). Turning on one ski is described under *Lift a Ski* in Chapter 5. If your ski tip is raised higher than the tail, your weight is too far back. If the tail is higher, your weight is too far forward. Alternate sides.

Then, link turns on one ski with the other ski removed. For this exercise and the following one ski exercises, permission to ski on one ski should be obtained from ski area management.

FIGURE 6.2 (top)

A verbal cue, such as "left foot, right foot" will help to establish rhythm and weight transfer.

ONE SKI AND ONE POLE. Use only one ski pole as you ski on one ski (FIGURE 6.4). Start with the pole that is on the same side of your body as your ski. The pole plant will help to start the more difficult turn: the turn on your inside ski. Alternate poles and skis.

FIGURE 6.3

Smoothly link turns with one ski off the snow.

FIGURE 6.4
Move smoothly from the outside edge to the inside edge.

FIGURE 6.5

Stay over the balance point on the sole of your foot.

ONE SKI AND NO POLES. Ski on one ski without poles (FIGURE 6.5). The hardest part about this exercise is getting started. Since it is easier to turn on your outside ski, make your first turn on that ski. Lean to the inside of the next turn as you pivot or steer your ski into that turn. It is helpful to establish a rhythm in order to continue turning. Alternate sides. ❊

SKILL DEVELOPMENT

TARGET SKIING. Aim your upper body down the hill toward a target such as a sign (FIGURE 6.6). Constantly face the target as you ski toward it. Keep your upper body quiet and turn your legs only. Transfer your weight from the outside ski of one turn to the outside ski of the next turn to time and coordinate your leg movements. Saying, "right foot, left foot," or, "right ski, left ski," in reference to weighting the appropriate outside foot/ski reinforces weight transfer and helps to establish a rhythm.

MOVING TARGET. On gentle terrain, ski short radius turns while following behind a partner (FIGURE 6.7). Have your partner ski in a wedge straight down the hill. Use your partner's back as an up-close target, and constantly face this target with your upper body.

FIGURE 6.6

Target skiing promotes a quiet upper body and an active lower body.

FIGURE 6.7
A leader provides a moving and up-close target to aim toward.

MOVEMENT DOWN THE HILL. Continue to move the body forward and down the hill at the start of a turn (FIGURE 6.8 a, b, c). The movement should coincide with the timing of the pole swing.

FIGURE 6.8 a, b, c (bottom)
As a reference, move over the balance point on the sole of the foot to start each turn.

FIGURE 6.9

*Use this exercise to
identify unnecessary upper
body movements.*

ARMS CROSSED. This exercise makes excessive upper body movements extremely apparent (FIGURE 6.9). Without your ski poles, cross your arms so that your hands touch your shoulders. Aim the cross of your arms at a target down the hill.

Strive for a countered, angulated position to correct the following errors:

(a) starting the turn with the upper body instead of with the legs

(b) leaning the upper body toward the center of the turn

(c) leaning and rotating toward the center of the turn

(d) bending forward at the waist

Continue to focus on lower body action as you uncross your arms and ski without poles. Then, add your ski poles.

FIGURE 6.10

*A tuck turn promotes effective
movements of the lower body.*

TUCK TURNS. *Tuck* turns develop strong rotary movements of the lower body which allow you to make quick turns. In the tuck position, the upper body is restricted, forcing the legs to control the skis (FIGURE 6.10).

Start in a high tuck position on gentle terrain. Aim your hands down the hill to direct your upper body. Turn slightly away from the fall line at first, then progress to greater changes of direction. It

is important to transfer weight to the new outside ski at the start of each turn. Progress to a lower tuck position, linking round, short radius turns.

Alternate tuck turns with short radius turns, retaining a stable upper body in both cases, as the lower body creates the turn.

FIGURE 6.12
Excessive upper body movement is restricted by your partner holding the pole.

HORIZONTAL POLE. Without ski poles, hold a Slalom pole horizontally in front of your body. Keep the pole level as you ski short radius turns straight down the hill. Tipping of the Slalom pole toward the inside of the turn indicates inward leaning of the upper body (FIGURE 6.11). Turning of the pole toward the center of the turn, indicates improper body rotation. The Slalom pole should stay level and not turn.

Try this exercise beside a partner (FIGURE 6.12). Each skier holds an end of the Slalom pole as pictured. The partner and the pole stabilize the upper bodies of both skiers. This exercise encourages active movement of the lower body.

HOLD HANDS. Practice this exercise with your partner on gen-

FIGURE 6.13

Keep your upper body quiet in order not to pull your partner off balance.

tle terrain. Hold hands lightly as you turn in the same direction at the same time (FIGURE 6.13). Establish a rhythm to help synchronize your movements. Do not rely on your partner for stability.

HOP TURNS. Hop turns develop strong lower body rotary movements of the legs underneath a non-turning upper body.

First, try hop turns without skis (FIGURE 6.14 a, b, c, d). Hop in place. Plant your right pole to turn to the right, plant your left pole to turn to the left. Use your pole plant to help you spring upward. Pole plants help support and stabilize the hopping action and set a rhythm. After you have added the pole action, hop for-

FIGURES 6.14 a, b, c, d
Keep your hips facing down the hill as you jump and turn your feet.

ward to move down the hill.

Next, try hop turns with one ski and then with the other ski (FIGURE 6.15 a, b, c, d). One-foot hop turns are easier to do than hop turns with both feet since there is less weight to lift and pivot.

With two skis, link rhythmic hop turns landing on and hopping off clean edges without skidding (FIGURE 6.16). Maintain a balanced body position as you face down the hill.

FIGURES 6.15 a, b, c, d
Hop on one ski to learn the movement pattern without the weight of two skis.

FIGURE 6.16
With two skis, jump off both feet and turn both feet at the same time.

HOP TURN ENTRY. This maneuver uses the strong lower body action developed in hop turns. At the start of a turn, pivot your skis slightly as you hop and turn both skis toward the fall line (FIGURE 6.17). Before the fall line, land on the edges of both skis with more weight on the outside ski of the turn. Ski through the end of the turn. Practice a hop turn entry in both directions, and then link turns. Then, evolve this exercise into smooth turns, without hopping. Replace the airborne rotary action with quick steering of the skis on the snow.

FIGURE 6.17
Hop off both feet to start a turn.

HOP TURNS ON THE OUTSIDE SKI. Hop turns from foot-to-foot strengthen your commitment to the outside ski. They are also beneficial for learning to get on and off your edges quickly. In addition, outside ski hop turns develop strong lower-body action beneath a quiet upper body.

First, try this exercise without skis (FIGURE 6.18 a, b, c, d). Stand with your feet turned slightly inward in a wedge position as you face down the hill. Hop off the inside edge of one foot and land on the inside edge of the other foot. Move your free leg next to the landing leg, but keep it off the snow. Continue hopping by alternating the push-off and landing feet. Press down on your right pole to help spring off your right foot, and press down on your left pole to help spring off your left foot.

FIGURES 6.18 a, b, c, d
*Keep your hips facing down the hill
as you jump from foot to foot.*

Next practice the exercise with skis (FIGURE 6.19). Then, lay two Slalom poles in the snow forming a "V" on *flat* terrain. Use the Slalom poles as guides for ski placement (FIGURE 6.20). Hop

FIGURE 6.19
Perform the same movement pattern with skis.

within the "V" with your skis parallel to the poles. Hop from the inside edge of one foot/ski to the inside edge of the other. Land with your left ski next to the left pole, and on the next hop, land with your right ski next to your right pole. On each hop, the free leg is brought parallel to the landing ski.

Practice outside foot hops moving down the hill without skis, and then try the same pattern of movements with skis.

Figure 6.20
Use Slalom poles as guides for ski placement.

HOP TURN ENTRY, OUTSIDE SKI. Apply the deliberate weight transfer in outside ski hop turns to short radius turns. At the completion of a turn, hop onto the inside edge of the new outside ski, directing it toward the fall line (FIGURE 6.21). Ski through the rest of the turn with the inside ski parallel to the outside ski. Link turns. Then, develop this exercise into a smooth turn entry with an early weight transfer (without hopping) and strong steering of the outside ski.

CHARLESTON. The *Charleston* is a fun and challenging variation of hop turns (FIGURE 6.22). First, try the *Charleston* without skis. Imagine a straight line on the snow in the fall line. Your left foot should land on the right side of this line and your right foot should land on the left side. Land on and hop off the outer edge of each boot. Point the toe of your boot slightly inward toward the center line in anticipation of the entire ski edge contacting the snow. Swing the free leg out to the side so that it will have momentum as it swings back under your body (FIGURE 6.23). This will help carry you to the other side of the "line." Plant the opposite pole from the ski you land on. When you have mastered the movements without skis, add your skis. As a ski lands on the snow, let it glide forward on edge momentarily to travel down the hill.

FIGURE 6.21

As you hop, tip and turn your ski in order to land on edge.

FIGURE 6.22 (bottom left)

Land on and jump off the outside edge of the inside ski.

FIGURE 6.23 (bottom right)

Kick the free leg out to the side.

REBOUND. Rebound can energetically propel a skier into the next turn.

In a carved turn, the outside ski is bent into an arc (*reverse camber*). When the pressure that bends the ski is released, the ski springs back, or "rebounds." The rebound, or release of stored energy in the ski, can be directed to propel you into the next turn.

In order to create rebound, stay on your outside ski a moment longer than usual. This will tighten the radius of your turn and increase pressure on your ski. After you rise very quickly for the next turn, your skis will flatten and the pressure will be released. The resultant release of energy helps your body continue to move upward, which lightens your skis on the snow, or actually pops you into the air. At this time, turn and tip your skis to be in position to continue the turn as you touch down.

SHORT TURNS ON A DIAGONAL. Ski continuous short radius turns while traveling diagonally down the hill (see *Garland Turns*, Chapter 4). Use the turn completion to work on the slicing action of the outside ski. Focus on the outside ski moving forward through the arc of the turn and not skidding out.

FORMATION SKIING. In formation skiing, two or more people ski together creating a pattern of turns. Participation in formation skiing promotes good rhythm and timing of movements as well as consistency and precision in performance. Descriptions of different formations follow.

(a) Synchronized Turns

In synchronized ("synchro") turns, two or more skiers turn

FIGURE 6.24
*Skiers turn in the same direction
at the same time.*

FIGURE 6.25

in the same direction at the same time (FIGURE 6.24). The rhythm, radius, and speed of the turns are the same. Synchronized turns can be performed in horizontal, vertical or diagonal relationships (FIGURE 6.25). The moment of pole touch can be used to signal the timing of synchronization.

FIGURE 6.26 (left)

*Usually, in opposite turn formation,
one skier is in the lead.*

(b) Opposite Turns

In opposite turns, skiers perform the same turns while skiing in opposite directions (FIGURE 6.26). The rhythm, radius and speed of the turns are the same, just the direction changes (FIGURE 6.27).

FIGURE 6.27 (right)

*Try to maintain a
consistent rhythm.*

FIGURE 6.28
The leader should choose a smooth path over the terrain.

(c) Lead-Follow

The follower skis in the leader's tracks (FIGURE 6.28). At first, focus on the leader's tracks in order to turn in the same place and not at the same time as the leader. With practice, you will be able to view the leader's movements but delay yours in order to start and complete each turn in his or her tracks. The size of the turns can be consistent or vary.

(d) Synchronized Speed Play

In this formation, speed is decreased, increased and maintained (FIGURE 6.29 a, b, c). Different ways to vary speed are described under *Speed* in Chapter 5.

One person skis consistent, rhythmic, short radius turns. Staying synchronized, another skier starts alongside, falls back, and then catches up to the consistent skier. Throughout the series of turns, both skiers start and end

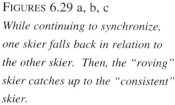

FIGURES 6.29 a, b, c
While continuing to synchronize, one skier falls back in relation to the other skier. Then, the "roving" skier catches up to the "consistent" skier.

FIGURE 6.30

The "roving" skier circles behind the "consistent" skier to change sides.

each turn at the same moment. The leader's pole plant provides a timing cue for the start of each turn.

(e) Synchronized Circle

This formation is a variation of *Synchronized Speed Play* (FIGURE 6.30). One person skis consistent, rhythmic, short radius turns. Staying synchronized, another skier circles behind and, then, advances to the other side of the consistent skier.

(f) Line Pull-out

The *Line Pull-out* is similar to the *Synchronized Circle*, but with four or more skiers. It provides yet another opportunity for skiers to practice short radius turns.

The skiers start in a vertical line and follow the leader's tracks (not synchronized). The leader skis consistent, rhythmic, short radius turns. After leading for a designated number of turns (six, for example), the leader pulls out to the side of the vertical line and the next-in-line becomes the leader for six turns. This process continues with each skier taking a turn at leading the line. When skiers pull away from the vertical line, they continue to turn, slowing their speed in order for the whole line to pass. Then they join the end of the line as the whole revolving process continues.

(g) Long and Short Medley

This pattern, consisting of different size turns, should be performed only by very competent skiers (FIGURE 6.31). In this formation, two skiers synchronize consistent, short radius turns in a vertical arrangement. They leave enough space for a third skier, performing long radius turns, to cross between them. ❄

FIGURE 6.31
This formation requires much precision.

SKI POLE ACTION

VERBAL CUE. For rhythmic turns, a verbal cue such as "touch" or "plant" helps to time the action of the pole.

POLE TIP FORWARD. Short radius turns allow no time for excessive arm movements that can hinder balance. Use wrist movement to bring the pole tip forward instead of moving your whole arm (FIGURE 6.32). After touching the pole in the snow, roll your hand downward with wrist action to pivot the pole off the snow. As one pole touches the snow, the other pole should be swinging forward.

ARM POSITION. Surveyor's ribbon provides an aid to keep your hands in front of your body and to restrict unnecessary arm movement (FIGURE 6.33). Use surveyor's ribbon since it will rip apart if

FIGURE 6.32
Swing the pole tip forward.

large arm movements become necessary to recover balance. It can be found at most hardware stores.

Hold your hands apart, several inches wider than the width of your body. Cut a piece of ribbon that is slightly longer than this measurement. Without your ski poles, wrap the ends of the tape around your hands. As you ski a series of short radius turns, aim the tape down the hill. Then, wrap the ends of the tape around the grips of your poles. The tape will restrict your hands from moving unnecessarily as you plant your poles (FIGURE 6.34).

FIGURE 6.33 (top)
Hold surveyor's ribbon to retain your arm position.

FIGURE 6.34
Use wrist movement primarily to plant your poles in short radius turns.

FIGURE 6.35 (top left)
Primarily use wrist action to plant your pole.

FIGURE 6.36 (right)
Ski beside a partner and copy the timing of his or her pole plant.

POLE TIMING. You can improve the rhythm and timing of your pole plants by skiing next to a competent partner (FIGURE 6.35, 36, 37). Synchronize turns on smooth terrain. Have your partner call out "plant" each time he/she plants a pole.

DOUBLE POLE PLANT. Planting both poles at the same time is an exercise to improve body position (FIGURE 6.38). It helps skiers:
- (a) get up and forward in order to be centered coming into a new turn
- (b) position both hands up and forward
- (c) maintain level shoulders
- (d) stabilize turning movements of the shoulders

FIGURE 6.37
Use a verbal cue such as "plant" or "right, left" to assist the timing of your pole plant.

To double pole plant, swing and touch the outside pole at the same time as you swing and touch the inside pole of the turn.

As a variation of the double pole plant, try planting both ski poles down the hill, below your skis (FIGURE 6.39). This exercise will help you to keep your upper body facing down the hill in short radius turns. Use wrist movement to touch the poles in and out of the snow quickly.

FIGURE 6.38
For a double pole plant, touch both poles at the same time.

ERROR CORRECTION AND DETECTION. Work with a partner to evaluate each other's pole plants. Look for symmetry of movement. Efficient and effective pole usage means eliminating any unnecessary hand, arm, and upper body movements. ❄

V**ARY TURNS.** Short radius turns can be different in shape, size and speed. Vary your turns as you ski.

TURN SHAPE

FIGURE 6.39
Touch both poles down the hill, below your skis.

SMOOTH TRANSITIONS. Include short and long radius turns in one run. In the transition from long turns to short turns, stay slightly longer on the outside ski to tighten the radius in preparation for short turns. Complete your last long turn across the hill, or even slightly up the hill in order to slow your speed. Face your upper body down the hill, as much as possible, before starting the first short radius turn.

In the transition from short to long radius turns, finish the last short turn closer to the fall line to gain speed. Aim your upper body toward the mid-way point of the arc for the longer radius turn.

RHYTHM CHANGES. Ski a series of turns that are consistent in rhythm, and then change the rhythm for the next series of turns. For example, alternate five medium radius turns with ten short radius turns. By choosing an odd number of turns in one radius, and an even number of turns in the other radius, transitions from one radius to the other will occur in both directions.

LEAD-FOLLOW. As the leader, vary the radius of your turns. As the follower, try to stay in the leader's tracks. ❉

TERRAIN AND SNOW CONDITIONS

ADAPT TO TERRAIN. Try to maintain rhythmic, short radius turns for a very long run, regardless of the terrain. This task encourages you to perform consistently, control your speed, and adapt to the demands presented by varying terrain.

VERSATILITY. To develop versatility, practice turns in all kinds of terrain including steeps, transitions, side hills and bumps, and in all kinds of snow conditions including ice, powder, and *crud* (see *Terrain and Snow Conditions*, Chapters 4 and 5).

STEEP TERRAIN. Skiers sometimes visualize their body position as perpendicular to the slope, but the correct stance is nearly vertical, balanced over the midpoints of their feet (FIGURE 6.40). Nevertheless, skiers often find their weight back when they start down steep terrain. This makes it difficult to turn and control speed. A short section of outside-ski hop turns can help you:

(a) find the balance point on the sole of your foot.

(b) create the strong rotary action that is necessary to turn your skis across a steep pitch and control your speed.

(c) commit to the outside ski of the turn in order not to lean up the hill. Leaning will decrease the weight on the outside ski and therefore, the ability to grip on a steep slope.

FIGURE 6.40

On steep terrain, stay over your balance point to keep your weight centered over your skis.

DEEP SNOW. The following *tactical* considerations are helpful for skiing deep snow:

    (a) ski rhythmic turns in, or close to the fall line (Figure 6.41)

    (b) start with shallow arcs

    (c) as speed increases, round-out the turns

    (d) ski steeper terrain to maintain speed

Also consider the following technical aspects:

    (a) distribute weight equally on both skis

    (b) assume a narrow stance, yet keep legs independent of each other

FIGURE 6.41

*Establish a rhythm
for your turns in deep snow.*

(c) use active flexion and extension movements

(d) face your upper body down the hill

(e) turn both skis at the same time with rotary action of the legs

CRUD SNOW. Since snow conditions are so changeable, concentrate on the balance point under your foot when you ski crud snow. Fore and aft adjustments are often necessary to ski smoothly through snow of different depths and densities.

BUMP SKIING. Skiing in the bumps promotes balance and the ability to adapt quickly to abrupt terrain changes. Elements to focus on include:

(a) keep your hands forward

(b) use a deliberate pole plant (FIGURE 6.42)

(c) look ahead to choose a line

(d) face your upper body down the hill

(e) press your ski tips down the back, steep side of bumps (or lift the tails of your skis to accomplish the same thing)

(f) maintain contact of the skis on the snow

(g) stay in the fall line

(h) ski long distances

FIGURE 6.42
The pole plant should be as light as possible, yet deliberate.

LINE IN THE BUMPS. There are many different approaches a skier can take in order to choose a path, or line in the bumps. Some of the variables involved are:

(a) the steepness of the hill

(b) the speed of descent

(c) the distance between bumps

(d) the shape of the bumps (round, sharp, drop-off)

(e) the depth of the troughs between bumps

As the pitch of the hill increases, speed control becomes more of a factor. Speed is decreased by turning the skis farther across the hill, increasing the edge angle, and/or minimizing the time in the fall line. You can choose to ski closer to the fall line, or to round-out your turns in order to ski faster or slower, respectively (FIGURE 6.43). Fast speed is more appropriate when bumps are far apart.

FIGURE 6.43

Skiing a round line that is close to the fall line.

When bumps are close together, turns are tighter and, therefore, slower speeds are appropriate.

Sharp bumps or drop-offs require more aggressive absorption movements of the legs in comparison to smooth, round-shaped bumps. Since your weight can get thrown forward or backward with abrupt terrain changes, constantly employ aggressive muscle action in the legs to return balance over the center of the ski. This is also essential for staying in balance when your skis accelerate quickly in a trough. The deeper the troughs, the less opportunity you have to determine where and when to turn.

The unpredictable nature of bumps requires a spontaneous combination of the following approaches, as well as tremendous quickness and balance. Look ahead to choose the smoothest line, and be ready to change your tactics as the terrain demands. Different tactics in the bumps include:

(a) turning sharply on the tops of bumps

(b) staying in the troughs

(c) turning on the banked side of bumps

(d) hitting the tops of the bumps

Turning sharply on the tops of bumps is a common way to begin bump skiing (see *Small Bumps*, Chapter 4). A relatively flat area on the uphill side, or top of each bump, provides room to turn and edge skis sharply. Speed is decreased in this way. Turning sharply on the bump is also used by highly-skilled bump skiers in order to slow their speed quickly.

Troughs are the carved-out channels between bumps. They often form a zig-zag pattern down the hill. As you cross the rise that separates one trough from the next, flex your legs to absorb the pressure that builds as your skis climb the rise. Then extend your legs into the trough, pressing your ski tips down to contact the snow. As your skis descend into the trough, they accelerate quickly and may get slightly ahead of your upper body. The deceleration of your skis at the transition between turns allows your upper body to re-center over your feet. There is less opportunity to check your speed when you ski through the troughs.

A smooth, round line can be skied by turning on the banked sides of bumps. Rather than being in the trough, the skier is above it, on the side of the adjacent bump. Ski across the top of the trough instead of turning into it. Then, turn on the side of the adjacent bump. Tighten the turn radius near the end of the turn in order to control speed and to be in position to start the next turn.

FIGURE 6.44

During a jump, keep your hands in front for balance.

In comparison, a straighter line can be skied by hitting the tops of the bumps and turning in the air. The skier lands on the bump with skis that are already redirected and edged to momentarily slow speed. For this approach, it is important that the skier be extended in flight in order to be in position to flex and absorb the impact of landing.

To jump safely in the bumps, it is essential to look ahead to the landing and ensure that it is clear of people and obstacles. Take off in a balanced position with ankles and knees flexed, and ready to spring. Extend your legs to lift off the jump in an upward and forward direction. Hold your hands in front of your body for stability (FIGURE 6.44). For the landing, a fairly tall stance is important so that your legs can bend to absorb the impact.

DIFFERENT PATHS. Start from different locations at the top of a bump run to explore different paths through the bumps.

ADJUST DIRECTION. Pre-determine a finish zone on the right or left side, or in the center at the bottom of a bump run. As you ski, work your way toward the particular finish zone that you have chosen. This challenge requires looking ahead and planning action instead of constantly reacting to terrain. ❄

LESSON PLAN

Select the exercises or subjects from each category that you would like to practice. Refer back to this outline to change your lesson plan for subsequent days.

WARM YOUR BODY. Refer to Chapter 9, *On the Snow Warm-up* for suggestions of exercises to warm and stretch your body.

RHYTHM AND REVIEW. Ski rhythmic, short radius turns on smooth terrain. Complete each turn sufficiently to maintain your speed. Focus on one of the following:
  (a) feet apart
  (b) "right foot, left foot" outside ski emphasis
  (c) both skis on the snow
  (d) upper body facing down the hill
  (e) hands in front
  (f) rhythmic pole plant
  (g) quick feet

DIRECTED FREE SKIING. Ski within the realm of short radius turns on intermediate, "blue" terrain. Short radius turns can be very round and tight, or less turny and close to the fall line. Select a topic from the previous list to keep in mind as you ski.

SCHOOLWORK. Select from the following exercises. Review the description and photographs earlier in this chapter that coincide with the titles you choose.

   (a) *Ski Without Poles*
   (b) *Ski on One Ski*
   (c) *One Ski and One Pole*
   (d) *One Ski and No Poles*
   (e) *Target Skiing*
   (f) *Moving Target*
   (g) *Arms Crossed*
   (h) *Tuck Turns*
   (i) *Horizontal Pole*
   (j) *Hold Hands*
   (k) *Hop Turns*
   (l) *Hop Turn Entry*
   (m) *Hop Turns on the Outside Ski*
   (n) *Hop Turn Entry, Outside Ski*
   (o) *Charleston*
   (p) *Rebound*
   (q) *Short Turns on a Diagonal*
   (r) *Formation Skiing*
   (s) *Ski Pole Action*

MOUNTAIN PLAYGROUND. Plan to ski steep slopes, over knolls and down bump runs. Look for challenging, yet non intimidating terrain. Play follow the leader with a friend and mix up the size of the turns.

SLOW AND EASY. Relax by "riding the edge" in longer radius turns.

LESSON PLAN EXAMPLE:

WARM YOUR BODY.
   (a) *Side Step Over Pole*
   (b) *Jump in Place*
   (c) *Knee to Elbow*
   (d) *Head Lean*

(e) *Arm Circle Variation*

(f) *Side Stretch*

(g) *Twisting Movements*

(h) *Inside Leg Stretch*

(i) *Tail Stretch*

(j) *Tip Stretch*

RHYTHM AND REVIEW.

(a) upper body facing down the hill

(b) rhythmic pole plant

DIRECTED FREE SKIING.

(a) "right foot, left foot" outside ski emphasis

(b) both skis on the snow

SCHOOLWORK.

(a) *Target Skiing*

(b) *Moving Target*

(c) *Arms Crossed*

(d) *Tuck Turns*

(e) *Horizontal Pole*

MOUNTAIN PLAYGROUND. Select bump runs, beginning on easier terrain and progressing to more difficult bumps.

SLOW AND EASY. Medium radius turns on smooth terrain. ❄

Power

CHAPTER 7:
STEP TURNS

This chapter covers step turns; parallel step, converging step and diverging step. The skills covered in the previous chapters provide the basis for step turns. The stepping action provides different options for the start of a turn. Step turns lead to versatile skiing—the ability to perform competently in varied terrain and conditions.

Step turns are dynamic parallel turns that begin with a parallel step, converging step or diverging step. Step turns allow you to change your path of descent quickly and efficiently. This is often necessary in a sport which has so many variables. It is helpful to have different turn options in order to meet the demands of changeable terrain, uneven surfaces, and inconsistent snow conditions. Also, stepping can be used to avoid obstacles and to move to preferable terrain.

This chapter is divided into three parts:

(a) Parallel Step Turns
(b) Converging Step Turns
(c) Diverging Step Turns ❄

PARALLEL
STEP TURNS

TURN DESCRIPTION. A parallel step is used to gain a slightly higher line (FIGURE 7.1). This may be necessary to change your line in the bumps or in a race course. A parallel step can also be used to change the position of the skis in relation to the body. With a step, the outside ski of the new turn is moved under the body and up the hill. This positions the body to the inside of the line the skis will travel through the arc of the new turn. It is an efficient way to acquire an edge early in the turn.

Parallel steps are suitable for both flat and steep terrain. A parallel step is less effective in deep snow conditions, where it is better to have weight distributed on both skis.

To start a parallel step turn, step the uphill ski laterally (sideways) up the hill. Place the stepped ski parallel to the downhill ski. Transfer your weight to the stepped ski, tip the ski onto its inside edge, and steer (or carve) it into the turn. Move the inside ski closer to the outside ski as you continue the dynamic parallel turn. The pole swing occurs with or after the step, and continues with the leg extension on the new outside ski, helping to direct the body into the

turn. The pole touch occurs when the outside ski tips onto its inside edge. Tipping of the ski refers to the movement from the uphill edge to flat and then to the downhill edge.

FIGURE 7.1

Parallel Step Turn

A parallel step is also known as an "inside/outside" or "inside/flat" move, referring to the edge usage. ❄

BALANCING EXERCISES

SIDE STEP OVER POLE. Stand beside a ski pole or a Slalom pole laid on the snow. Step the ski that is closest to the pole over the pole and stand on it momentarily before bringing it back to its original place. Move this ski back and forth over the pole to practice a parallel step, weight transfer, and balance on one ski (FIGURE 7.2).

FIGURE 7.2

Step repeatedly over your ski pole to practice a parallel step.

STEP DRILLS. Lay three or more Slalom poles on the snow in the fall line or in a traverse on nearly flat terrain. Step one ski over the first pole and then the other ski. Step far enough sideways to allow room for the second ski. Cross back and forth over the poles in this manner as you ski parallel to the poles (FIGURE 7.3).

Lay several Slalom poles along a traverse line with each succeeding pole set about twelve inches up the hill. Starting in a traverse on the downhill side of the first pole, step uphill over the pole with both skis to ski a traverse line below the second pole. Step over that pole and repeat for each succeeding pole. ❄

SKILL DEVELOPMENT

STEP IN A TRAVERSE. As you traverse across the hill, step from foot to foot (FIGURE 7.4). Balance and glide on one ski before stepping to the other ski.

PARALLEL STEP. As you traverse across the hill, step your

FIGURE 7.3

Step back and forth over poles.

FIGURE 7.4
*Practice transferring your weight
from one foot to the other as you
lift your legs in a stepping motion.*

uphill ski up the hill and momentarily place it *parallel* to the position of the downhill ski. Then return the uphill ski to its original position. Repeatedly step in this manner (FIGURE 7.5). Practice this exercise while crossing the hill in both directions.

PARALLEL STEP GARLAND. *Parallel Step Garlands* can be used for the repetitive practice of steering the skis down the hill after a parallel step occurs (see *Garland Turns*, Chapter 4). Start in a traverse. Step up the hill, weight the uphill ski, and steer both skis slightly down the hill. Before reaching the fall line, transfer weight to your original downhill ski. Finish in a turn continuing in the

FIGURE 7.5

Practice the parallel step
repeatedly.

direction of your initial traverse. Repeatedly step and turn in this manner while crossing the hill in both directions (FIGURE 7.6).

FIGURE 7.6
Parallel Step Garland

TRAVERSE, STEP AND TURN. Starting in a traverse, perform a parallel step up the hill. The stepped ski becomes the outside ski of a turn as you weight this ski and steer both skis through the entire turn. Link traverses, parallel steps and turns.

STEP AND TURN. Decrease the length of the traverse between turns until the completion of one turn leads into the parallel step turn entry of the next turn.

REVIEW.   Review and practice *Upper Body Direction* and *Floaters*, Chapter 5.   The movement patterns described in these exercises are applicable to parallel step turns.   *Floaters* use a weight transfer without a step, but are otherwise similar to *Parallel Step Turns*.

VARY RADIUS. Practice a parallel step in short, medium and-long radius turns to become proficient in this maneuver. ❄

TURN DESCRIPTION. In converging step turns, the outside ski is directed toward the fall line early in the turn, cutting off the top of the turn. A converging step is used to move quickly into the fall line and onto the inside edge of the new outside ski (FIGURE 7.7). Converging step turns can be used on all terrain. They are effective on very steep terrain where it is necessary to minimize the time spent turning into the fall line in order to

FIGURE 7.7

Converging Step Turn

get the skis quickly across the hill to control speed. A converging step turn is very effective for getting started in deep snow and on steep terrain.

To start a converging step turn, move the uphill ski to create a converging relationship with ski tips together and tails apart. This action is called "*stemming*." Move from the inside edge of your downhill ski (of the previous turn) to the inside edge of your new uphill ski (new outside ski). The converging action points your ski down the hill. Step onto an edged ski. The pole swing coincides with the stemming action and the pole touches as the inside edge engages. Bring the inside ski parallel and complete the turn as a dynamic parallel turn.

A converging step is also known as an "inside/inside" move or "stem step," referring to the edge usage. ❄

BALANCING EXERCISES

CONVERGING STEPS IN A CIRCLE. On flat terrain, step your ski tails around in a circle, pivoting around the tips of your skis (FIGURE 7.8). Step from the inside edge of one ski to the inside edge of the other ski. Repeat, stepping in

FIGURE 7.8

Pivot around the tips of your skis to step in a circle.

Figure 7.9

Step over the spokes of the wagon wheel to practice converging steps.

the other direction.

WAGON WHEEL. On flat terrain, lay eight Slalom poles on the snow with one end of all of the poles touching to form the spokes of a wagon wheel. Step over each pole as described in *Converging Steps in a Circle*, facing the center of the wheel (FIGURE 7.9).

ZIG-ZAG DRILL. Set this course close to the fall line, on nearly flat terrain. Lay poles at angles on the snow (FIGURE 7.10). Step to cross over each pole as you reach the junction between poles. The outside ski must be stemmed in order to place it parallel to the pole. ✳

FIGURE 7.10

As you step over the first pole, point the lifted ski in the direction the second pole lies. Set your ski down to run parallel to this pole. (Start with a course in which the poles are arranged at less of an angle.)

SKILL DEVELOPMENT

CONVERGING STEP. As you traverse across the hill, stem your uphill ski, touching it *lightly* on the snow. After each stem, return the uphill ski to its original position (FIGURE 7.11). Repeatedly step in this manner (FIGURE 7.12). Practice this exercise while crossing the hill in both directions.

CONVERGING STEP GARLAND. *Converging Step Garlands* can be used for the repetitive practice of starting into a turn after the converging step occurs (see *Garland Turns*, Chapter 4). Start in a traverse. Stem the uphill ski up the hill, weight the uphill ski, and carve slightly down the hill with skis parallel. Before reaching the fall line, transfer weight to your original downhill ski, but without a step. Finish in a turn in order to continue in the direction of your

FIGURE 7.11

Keep the upper body steady as you step your uphill ski.

FIGURE 7.12
*Practice the converging step
repeatedly.*

initial traverse. Repeatedly stem and turn in this manner while
crossing the hill in both directions (FIGURE 7.13).

TRAVERSE, STEM AND TURN. Start in a traverse. Stem and
weight the uphill ski to carve a turn. Link traverses with converging step turns.

STEM AND TURN. Decrease the length of the traverse between
turns until the completion of one turn leads into the stem entry of
the next turn, leaving out the traverse.

FALL LINE CONVERGING TURNS. To develop quick converging steps in the fall line, practice *Outside Ski Hop Turns*, Chapter 6. Follow this exercise with short radius turns, starting each turn by hopping onto the inside edge of the newly stemmed outside ski. Let this exercise evolve into quick converging step turns by stepping instead of hopping onto the outside ski. ❊

FIGURE 7.13
Converging Step Garland

TURN DESCRIPTION. A diverging step is used to gain a higher line, particularly in a race course (FIGURE 7.14). A diverging step is also effective for removing pressure from the outside ski. When weight is transferred onto the flatter inside ski, there is less resistance, allowing the ski to glide faster. Diverging step turns are more appropriate on moderate terrain where turn completion on the outside ski is not essential for speed control.

DIVERGING STEP TURNS

FIGURE 7.14

Diverging Step Turn

Before the completion of a dynamic parallel turn, pivot the inside ski across the hill. This creates a diverging relationship with ski tails together and tips apart. Step onto the uphill edge of this inside ski. The pole swing occurs with or after the step, and continues with the leg extension on the new outside ski, helping to direct the body into the turn. The pole touch occurs when the new outside ski tips onto the inside edge. Bring the inside ski parallel and continue the turn as a dynamic parallel turn.

The diverging step is also known as an "inside/outside" move, referring to the edge usage.

A common variation of the diverging step turn incorporates the divergent relationship without the stepping action. In this turn, transfer weight to the inside ski and steer the inside ski to complete the turn. This ski will then become the outside ski of the next turn. Weight is transferred without a stepping action. ❆

BALANCING EXERCISES

DIVERGING STEPS IN A CIRCLE. On flat terrain, step your ski tips around in a circle, pivoting around the tails of your skis (FIGURE 7.15). Step from the inside edge

FIGURE 7.15

Pivot around the tails of your skis to step in a circle.

FIGURE 7.16

Step over the spokes of the wagon wheel to practice diverging steps.

of one ski to the outside edge of the other ski. Repeat, stepping in the other direction.

WAGON WHEEL. Lay eight Slalom poles on the snow with one end of all of the poles touching to form the spokes of a wagon wheel. Face the outside of the wheel and step over each pole as described in *Diverging Steps in a Circle* (FIGURE 7.16). ✳

SKILL DEVELOPMENT

FALL LINE SKATE. Skate down the fall line of a gentle hill (FIGURE 7.17). Push off with the inside edge of one ski and move your upper body over the other ski as you glide on its outside edge. Bring your feet together before pushing off onto the other ski (see *Skating*, Chapter 4).

SKATE RACE. You can practice diverging steps with a partner in a race across flat terrain (FIGURE 7.18). This skating exercise

FIGURE 7.17
Skate down the hill.

helps develop a deliberate weight transfer off an edged ski.

FALL LINE SKATE AND TURN. After gliding onto the outside edge as described in the *Fall Line Skate* exercise, tip your ski onto the inside edge and steer it into a shallow turn. Finish with your skis parallel, ready to skate into the next turn.

STEEP TRAVERSE, SKATE AND TURN. Start from a steep traverse. Skate onto the outside edge of your uphill ski and then steer it into the turn. Practice this turn in both directions.

SKATE AND TURN. Link turns so that the completion of one turn leads into the skate entry of the next turn.

STEER THE INSIDE FOOT. Without skis, draw an arc in the snow with the outside edge of the inside foot of the turn. Concentrate on the steering action of the foot. Try to capture this same feeling and action while skiing.

EARLY WEIGHT TRANSFER. In a turn, actively steer the inside ski in a tighter arc than the outside ski. Then, transfer your weight to this ski before the turn is completed. It becomes the outside ski of the new turn. Bring the inside ski parallel and continue in a dynamic parallel turn.

EXTENSION. Extend your leg on the gliding, inside ski, as you move in the direction of the upcoming turn. The extension flattens the ski, making it easier to steer or tip into the next turn. ❋

LESSON PLAN

Select the exercises or subjects from each category that you would like to practice. Refer back to this outline to change your lesson plan for subsequent days.

WARM YOUR BODY. Refer to Chapter 9, *On the Snow Warm-up* for suggestions of exercises to warm and stretch your body.

RHYTHM AND REVIEW. Before jumping into step turns, establish rhythmic parallel turns. In preparation for step turns, focus on one of the following:
(a) linked round arcs that are completed across the hill
(b) deliberate weight transfer from one ski to the other
(c) stay on the outside ski throughout the turn
(d) quiet upper body

DIRECTED FREE SKIING. Start on smooth, gentle terrain so that you can concentrate on the movement patterns without being thrown off balance by terrain. Then, progress to more difficult terrain. Work on a particular step long enough to feel comfortable with the maneuver. Focus on the angle the stepped ski is placed on the snow.

SCHOOLWORK. Select from the following exercises. Review the description and photographs earlier in this chapter that coincide with the titles you choose.

Parallel Step:
   (a) *Side Step Over Pole*
   (b) *Step Drills*
   (c) *Step in a Traverse*
   (d) *Parallel Step*
   (e) *Parallel Step Garland*
   (f) *Traverse, Step and Turn*
   (g) *Step and Turn*

Converging Step:
   (a) *Converging Steps in a Circle*
   (b) *Wagon Wheel*
   (c) *Zig-Zag Drill*
   (d) *Converging Step*
   (e) *Converging Step Garland*
   (f) *Traverse, Stem and Turn*
   (g) *Stem and Turn*
   (h) *Fall Line Converging Turns*

Diverging Step:
   (a) *Diverging Steps in a Circle*
   (b) *Wagon Wheel*
   (c) *Fall Line Skate*
   (d) *Skate Race*
   (e) *Fall Line Skate and Turn*
   (f) *Steep Traverse, Skate and Turn*
   (g) *Skate and Turn*
   (h) *Steer the Inside Foot*
   (i) *Early Weight Transfer*
   (j) *Extension*

MOUNTAIN PLAYGROUND. Explore step turns in a variety of terrain. Use converging steps on steep terrain, diverging steps on moderate terrain and parallel steps on any terrain. Avoid step turns in powder or crud snow conditions. Alternate dynamic parallel turns with different step turns and vary the radius of the turns.

SLOW AND EASY. Return to parallel turns by shifting weight onto the new outside ski without stepping.

LESSON PLAN EXAMPLE:

WARM YOUR BODY.
    (a) *Side Step Over Pole*
    (b) *Run in Place*
    (c) *One Ski Scooter*
    (d) *Head Lean*
    (e) *Arm Circle Variation*
    (f) *Side Stretch*
    (g) *Twisting Movements*
    (h) *Inside Leg Stretch*
    (i) *Calf Stretch*
    (j) *Tip Stretch*

RHYTHM AND REVIEW.
    (a) deliberate weight transfer from one ski to the other
    (b) stay on the outside ski throughout the turn

DIRECTED FREE SKIING. Focus on the angle the stepped ski is placed on the snow.

SCHOOLWORK.

Parallel Step:
    (a) *Step in a Traverse*
    (b) *Parallel Step*
    (c) *Parallel Step Garland*
    (d) *Traverse, Step and Turn*
    (e) *Step and Turn*

MOUNTAIN PLAYGROUND. Alternate dynamic parallel turns with step turns and vary the radius of the turns.

SLOW AND EASY. Ski smooth parallel turns keeping both skis on the snow at all times. ❄

CHAPTER 8: DEEP SIDECUT CARVE

Extreme Arcs

Deep Sidecut Carve

183

CHAPTER 8:
DEEP SIDECUT CARVE

Deep sidecut skis provide virtually every skier an exciting opportunity to learn to carve turns. Deep sidecut skis offer truly enhanced skiing pleasure, not merely cosmetic changes. In this chapter, a detailed progression will lead you through a smooth transition from traditional skis to deep sidecut skis. The *Direct Carve Progression* will help you carve turns more effectively.

We suggest you use shorter length skis, such as 150 centimeter carving skis, to progress more quickly. The carving action is very apparent with this length since the sidecut scribes a small turn radius. Feelings and related sensations are more distinct. ❋

FIGURE 8.1

A carved turn on deep sidecut skis

DEEP SIDECUT TECHNIQUE

Why carve? Carving is the most efficient way to control a turn. You are in command when your ski grips the surface of the snow and your edge holds a curved path. Slipping or skidding sideways, particularly over uneven terrain or surface conditions, is less secure. In a carved turn, it is the shape of the turn—the roundness and the extent of the turn—that controls the speed of descent. One could argue that the greatest skiers on the mountain are the skiers that carve the cleanest turns.

Compared to traditional skis, these skis allow you to accomplish carved turns at slower speeds and with less physical effort than before. When a carved turn tightens, the *centrifugal* force increases even without the addition of increased speed. Sensing these forces as you zing through a turn provides a thrill reminiscent of high speed racing turns (FIGURE 8.1).

Deep sidecut skis tend to be skied at shorter lengths than traditional skis. The typical ten centimeter difference makes them easier to turn. When the edge is engaged, as in a carved turn, they are surprisingly stable, even at very high speeds.

When used properly, the attributes of deep sidecut ski design can help skiers progress more quickly, ski with less effort, and ski more terrain successfully. To prepare for the *Direct Carve Progression,* review the following:

BALANCE POINT. To bend a ski into a true circular arc requires that your weight is concentrated at a specific point along the length of the ski. It is called the *balance point.* This point serves as a reference for pressuring the ski most effectively. With deep sidecut skis, the balance point is at the middle of the foot. This coincides with the mid-flex point of the ski. Additionally, weight is focused in a turn on the inner side of the foot (the outside foot/ski of the turn).

The location of the balance point is the same for deep sidecut and traditional skis. But, with less sidecut, it is necessary to adjust pressure more deliberately in order to weight the ski tip to start the turn, the center of the ski to move through the arc, and the tail to control the completion of the turn. With a deeper sidecut ski, the hourglass shape causes the flared tip and tail to cut into the snow when the ski is tilted on edge (refer to model). As a result, it is not

Deep Sidecut Carve

necessary to pressure the tip and tail heavily. The ski will continue in the intended arc with minimal fore and aft movement. Since movement from the balance point is not as exacting, deep sidecut skis tend to be more forgiving.

In actuality, moving off the balance point does occur. Some aft movement is a result of body flexion which causes the center of mass to move slightly back through the completion of the turn. Or, the skier may choose to pressure toward the heel of the foot and reduce the *edge angle* to alter the radius of the turn (wider arc). In these situations, pressure may range from the ball of the foot to the middle of the foot as the turn progresses. But, it is important to begin each new turn with weight over the middle of the foot.

What happens when weight moves toward the heel of the foot? Typically, the radius of the turn widens since the edge angle of the ski on the snow decreases. Also, a larger body movement forward is necessary to weight and engage the tip of the ski for the next turn. As a result, the skier may be late in setting up the turn and, therefore, carving may not be established early in the turn.

WIDE STANCE. Since the tips and tails of deep sidecut skis are considerably wider than traditional skis, it is natural that skiers would place their feet further apart (FIGURE 8.2). It is easier to balance in a wider stance. A wide stance (feet approximately hip width apart) allows room to tip the outside ski onto a steep angle.

FIGURE 8.2
Skis are apart. Both skis are weighted, but with a greater portion of weight on the outside ski.

In a narrow stance, the inside leg inhibits the inward lean of the outside leg as the edge angle increases. (See *Tip the Ski* in the first chapter, *A Curved Path*.) A wide stance complements the active roles played by both skis in a carved turn. Therefore, a wide stance is the normal position on deep sidecut skis.

TWO SKIS. Although the outside ski remains the principal ski in every turn, the inside ski has become more active than before (FIGURE 8.2). This is possible because the majority of the skier's weight is no longer necessary to bend the outside ski into an arc. Deep sidecut skis are softer and easier to flex into a deep arc with less muscular effort. Thus, more weight can be carried on the inside ski. Just as balance is easier on two feet than one, it is easier to ski with two skis on the snow. The increase of ski surface with two skis solidly on the snow is also beneficial for stability at high speeds, especially considering the shorter lengths of deep side cut skis.

BODY ANGLES. Deep sidecut skis are meant to be skied on edge, taking advantage of the ski's design.

Lateral movements of the body are elongated with the tight radius turns made with these skis (FIGURE 8.3). As turns tighten, centrifugal force increases, pulling the skier to the outside of the

FIGURE 8.3

Reaching the skis out to the side

FIGURE 8.4

The inside ski leads through a turn.

FIGURE 8.5

When the circular arc starts at the very beginning of the turn, the skis aim straight down the hill at the mid-point of the arc.

turn. Greater inward lean, particularly of the lower body, is necessary to counter the unbalancing effect of centrifugal force. The lower body inclines as the angle of the ski increases in relation to the slope of the hill. This creates lateral angles of the body, particularly at the hip (hip angulation) as the lower body leans inward and the upper body remains relatively vertical.

The sensation the skier acquires is often described as *reaching the skis out to the side.*

INSIDE SKI LEAD. *Lead ski* refers to the forward movement, or lead, of the inside ski of the turn in relation to the position of the outside ski (FIGURE 8.4). Forward movement of the inside ski is vital for smooth transitions between turns. The advancement of the inside ski is a smooth continuous movement that begins as weight is transferred to the outside ski, and increases as the turn progresses. The movement ends when the inside ski becomes the outside ski of the new turn.

The amount of ski lead coincides with the orientation of the body through a turn. Inside ski lead is one aspect of a *countered* and *angulated* stance that inhibits the tails of the skis from skidding, and directs the upper body toward the next turn.

TURN SHAPE. The shape of a turn reflects the design characteristics of the ski. Usually, the deeper the sidecut, the sharper a ski will carve a turn. A shorter ski will turn in a tighter arc compared to a longer ski of the same tip, waist and tail dimensions. A softer ski will bend into a deeper arc more easily than a comparatively stiffer ski.

Once in a carve, the characteristics of the ski tend to keep it turning in a smooth arc. Since the skis are edged and not pivoted at the beginning of the turn, the circular shape of the turn starts immediately. At the mid-point of the arc, the ski should aim straight down the hill (FIGURE 8.5). Increasing the edge angle contributes to a tighter radius turn. ❋

Pure carving is accomplished by weighting and angulating a ski so that it bends into a circular arc. Deep sidecut skis are designed to make as perfect a carved turn as possible. The following progression is specific to learning or optimizing carving skills.

In each of the following exercises, strive to use the design of the ski to leave narrow, carved arcs in the snow. Refer to Chapter 1, *A Curved Path*, to review carving.

TRAVERSE POSITION. Begin in a traverse to feel the circular arc that results from edging and weighting a deep sidecut ski. Work toward perfection of traverse exercises to hone your edging and carving skills.

To review the traverse position, stand across a gentle slope with your feet about hip width apart. Move your body forward to feel your weight concentrated behind the big toe of the ball of your downhill foot, and behind the little toe on your uphill foot. Assume a tall, *square position* in which your ski tips are even and your body faces in the direction of your skis (FIGURE 8.6). Then, bend both legs and slide your uphill ski forward. Let the uphill side of your body move forward naturally, into the traverse position. With this action, the upper body faces more down the hill and more weight shifts to the inside edge of the downhill ski. Increase the weight along the inside of your foot to increase the edge angle. A hip angulated position occurs (FIGURE 8.7). Your lower legs should stay in contact with the fronts of your boots. This contact is an essential part of correct form since it enforces your forward position above the balls of your feet (FIGURE 8.8).

TRAVERSE USING SIDECUT. From a traverse, tip both skis onto uphill edges. Each ski should track and not slip or skid sideways, losing the edge. Your tracks will be curved in the uphill direction as a result of the sidecut of the skis. A portion of a turn occurs. Alter the angle of the ski's edge on the snow to change the radius of the turn. A relatively flat ski will leave a shallow arc in comparison to a ski that is tipped onto a steeper edge.

As the edge angle changes, angulation helps to maintain bal-

DIRECT CARVE PROGRESSION

FIGURE 8.6 and FIGURE 8.7
Move from a square body position (top) to a traverse position (bottom).

ance. Angulation shifts the center of mass of the body toward the center of a turn, thereby compensating for the unbalancing effect of centrifugal force. In an angulated position, the upper body stays relatively vertical, while the lower body (hip angulation) or the lower legs (knee angulation) are at a slant to the snow. Angulation generally occurs with countering movements. In a countered position, the skier's outside hip is rotated slightly back in relation to the inside hip. Or, in terms of a traverse, the downhill hip is slightly back in relation to the uphill hip. The upper body remains parallel to the hips, so it slightly faces toward the downhill direction. Together, a countered and hip-angulated stance inhibits the tails of the skis from skidding. (FIGURE 8.9)

FIGURE 8.9

Use the sidecut of your skis to draw a curved arc in the snow.

TRAVERSE EXERCISES. Repeatedly practice the following exercises across the hill moving in both directions. Begin with a

shallow traverse on a gentle slope. Progress to steeper traverse *lines*.

    (a) Begin a traverse in a square stance. Slide the uphill ski forward and back to differentiate between a body position in which the uphill ski leads, and a square body position in which the skis are even. Bend your legs and maintain contact with the fronts of your boots as you advance the ski. Rise to return to a square position.

    (b) Experiment with edging and slipping movements. From a traverse, flatten your skis by tipping your feet slightly down the hill until your edges lose their grip and slip. Then, increase edging by tipping the skis up the hill to recover your traverse.

    (c) In a traverse, explore the turn radii that result from more edge and less edge. Compare the long radius that occurs with minimal edging to the shorter radii that occur as edging increases.

FIGURE 8.10

Ski a progressively steeper line until you begin straight down the hill.

TURN COMPLETION. Ski a series of traverses using the sidecut of the skis to develop a carved turn completion. At the start of each traverse, aim your skis a little more down the hill (FIGURE 8.11). Proceed in this manner until you start with your skis pointing straight down the hill (FIGURE 8.10). Continue the carved turn until your skis point across the hill.

FIGURE 8.11

This illustrates curved paths progressing from a sidecut traverse to the finish of a turn.

EDGE CHANGE. Skiing a carved turn requires that the skis are tipped onto edges at the very start of the turn. The following exercises rehearse the tipping movement of both feet/skis. The last exercise incorporates tipping movements to connect turns.

    (a) Stand in front of a mirror to check your movements as you practice tipping your feet from side to side. Place the back of a chair on each side to aid your balance. Practice with and without your ski boots. Press both knees forward and to the side as you tip your feet. Concentrate your weight on the head of the first metatarsal behind your big toe on the outside foot. Also weight the area behind your little toe on your inside foot. Your lower legs should contact but not

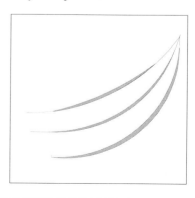

Deep Sidecut Carve

FIGURE 8.12 and FIGURE 8.13
Tip your feet to create edge change.

FIGURE 8.14 and FIGURE 8.15
Balance over the inside edge of the outside foot. Feel your weight along the inside of the foot. It should be a strong sensation.

press against the fronts of your boots (FIGURE 8.12 and FIGURE 8.13).

(b) As you change edges, concentrate on the position of your whole body. Angulate your body to balance over the inside edge of your outside foot for each edge change (FIGURE 8.14 and FIGURE 8.15).

(c) Use the chairs or your poles as a support in order to feel how your body moves toward the inside of the turn as you tip

your skis at the start of the turn (FIGURE 8.16).

(d) On smooth, nearly flat terrain, complete a parallel turn in a wide stance. Then, flatten your skis, and tip them onto their opposite edges to start turning down the hill (FIGURE 8.17). Be very patient with this transition between turns. Since you are moving at a slow speed on gentle terrain, it will take some time for the sidecut of the ski to scribe an arc in the snow. Make sure your feet are apart as you tip both skis in the same direction. Look at your tracks to confirm sharp impressions of angulated skis. A broader swath of disturbed snow is caused by a skidding action, in contrast to the sharp track of a carved turn.

LINK CARVED TURNS. On gentle terrain, apply the edge change movements of the previous exercise to linked turns (FIGURE 8.18). Aim your upper body at a point down the hill. Standing with your feet apart, tip your skis slightly onto their edges to scribe a shallow arc before changing edges. Both skis should be flat on the snow between tipping movements in opposing directions.

FIGURE 8.16

The body moves toward the center of the turn as you create edging.

FIGURE 8.17

Tip onto new edges to start the next turn. Use extreme patience.

Deep Sidecut Carve

Concentrate on the lead of the inside ski to make the transition between turns easier and to make the transition smoother. Your left ski should lead to turn to the left. Your right ski should lead to turn to the right.

MILES. To become competent with linked sidecut turns practice for miles and miles on smooth, gentle terrain. Then challenge your edging ability by varying the radius within the realm of medium and long turns. Explore:

    (a) minimizing edging to draw out the turn

    (b) tipping your skis higher on edge to accomplish a sharper turn

    (c) alternating turns of different radii, i.e.: three long turns with five medium turns

    (d) changing edges slowly, changing edges quickly

    (e) skiing over uneven terrain

As you take run after run, keep in mind:

(a) balance point on the foot

(b) skis apart

(c) edges tip concurrently on both skis

(d) the lead of your left ski when you turn to the left, the lead of your right ski when you turn to the right

(e) upper body maintains a comfortable position over the balance point, facing in the general direction of down the hill

DIAGONAL DESCENT. At this stage of development, you may come to terrain that is too steep to manage a carved turn comfortably. In a precise transition from edge to edge, speed increases quickly. If the start of a turn is rushed, skidding will occur. Therefore, until tighter turns are mastered, approach steeper terrain at a diagonal. Link carved turns diagonally across the hill so that speed does not build too quickly (FIGURE 8.19).

Rather than skiing in the *fall line*, ski toward a point diagonally down the hill. Begin carved turns and stop when you have crossed the hill. Change direction with a quick *pivot slip* (Chapter 4) to get set to go in the other direction. Continue descending diagonally down the hill in these alternating directions (FIGURE 8.20).

Progress to linking each diagonal descent with a turn. Your skis will accelerate as they are tipped down the hill into the turn. Continue to weight the outside ski to keep turning until you are headed slightly up the hill. This will decrease your speed and you can proceed diagonally with sidecut turns.

ROUND ARC. Ski a rounder turn through the fall line by staying longer on the skis to continue the arc before beginning the upcoming turn (FIGURE 8.21). Let the arc be nearly 180 degrees, or half a circle. As you begin a new turn, gradually tip the skis farther to increase the edge angle and the "bite" into the snow. Progressively shift weight to the outside ski as centrifugal force builds. After half the turn, as your skis turn away from the fall line, flex your body by bending the ankles, knees and torso to reduce downward pressure on the skis. Then, just before the next turn, begin to apply weight to the inside ski, to help transfer the weight to the next out-

FIGURE 8.19

Tip your feet to create edge change while crossing a hill.

FIGURE 8.20

Ski in a diagonal direction to cross
a steep hill.

side ski for a smooth transition between turns.

INCREASE SPEED. Ski fast on gentle terrain to feel your skis work (FIGURE 8.22). Link long radius turns, staying close to the fall line to maintain speed. When you increase your speed, the sensation of slicing through the snow becomes stronger. The relationship between the edging angle of the ski on the snow surface and the radius of the turn become more apparent. Longer radius arcs are achieved with less edge angle than shorter radius arcs. Smaller segments of the circle maintain a path closer to the fall line than larger segments of the circle.

It is important to judge your surroundings before going faster. First, ski slowly to read the terrain. Look for wide open slopes with smooth terrain, few skiers, and natural run-outs without obstacles. If your speed becomes too great, slow down by continuing a round carved turn until you are traveling uphill.

FIGURE 8.21

Stay with the turn longer to round out the arc.

FIGURE 8.22

Look for wide open spaces in which to increase your speed.

At the beginning of a carved turn, the skis are not pivoted at all. Instead, the skis move toward the fall line in an edged arc, gaining speed. When speed increases, pressure on the skis increases, too, as a result of centrifugal force. The pressure contributes to the bend of the outside ski, and the edging angle determines the radius of the arc carved by the ski.

DYNAMIC CARVED TURNS. Dynamic turns are all about managing the pressure that causes an edged ski to bend and carve, and using the resultant energy to carry you into the next turn (FIGURE 8.23). Tightly carved turns occur when edge angle is increased, especially if coupled with speed. When you slide along a straight path at constant speed, the total force exerted by your body on the ski is your body weight. When you deviate from a straight path to a curved path, the change in forces produces an increase of pressure on the ski. The sharper and faster the turn, the greater the added pressure contributed by centrifugal force. Therefore, your efforts are largely aimed at managing, and not creating pressure.

The centrifugal force pushing your body outwards adds to your downward body force. The snow reacts to the combined force by pressing inwards and upwards by an equal amount against the ski. This force of the snow is distributed along the length of the ski and bends the ski into a relatively tight arc. In technical terms, the distributed force is called pressure—the pressure between the ski and the snow. Bending of the ski increases as the pressure increases. The total amount of pressure is effected by snow depth and density.

A dynamic turn begins from a low position as a result of flexing the body to help reduce pressure at the end of the previous turn. The body continues to move down the hill as the legs extend to the outside and the skis are tipped onto edge. An angulated and countered position occurs early in the turn as the skis chart a wider course than the upper body. The skier's weight, the extra pressure exerted by the skier as he/she extends against the ski, and the centrifugal force of the turn all create pressure on the edged ski. Therefore, the ski bends into an arc very early in the turn. The forces continue to bend the edged ski, continuing the circular arc.

In a pure carved turn, the radius of the arc is controlled by the edging angle, as demonstrated by the model discussed in Chapter 1, A Curved Path. Thus, increased pressure in the second half of the turn does not change the radius, but instead, it tends to cause skidding out of the arc. This is countered by "giving in"—bending at the ankles, knees and torso to reduce the excess pressure. The upper body continues to move along a smooth path as the legs extend into the next turn, repeating the movement pattern.

Deep Sidecut Carve

FIGURE 8.24

The skis are to the outside of the upper body at the start of the turn.

The farther away your skis are from your upper body at the beginning of a turn, the more they will be tipped on edge. The greater the edge angle, the more pressure there will be on the ski early in the turn. The greater the pressure is early in the turn, the more the ski will bend into an arc and carve a tight turn (FIGURE 8.24).

The inside leg must bend sufficiently to compensate for its higher position on an inclined surface. The inside ski will advance as the leg is flexed due to body anatomy. The lead of the inside leg can help to maintain the skier in a forward stance when the lower leg is kept in contact with the front of the boot. Since the inside ski is not as heavily weighted as the outside ski, it cannot bend into as deep an arc or carve as tight a radius. Therefore, the inside ski must be steered, to some degree.

As you work on dynamic carved turns, try the following:

(a) Experiment with how far you can reach your skis away from your body at the start of a turn. Be aware that it is a common mistake to raise straight upward instead of continuing body movement down the hill as you extend your legs.

(b) Be soft in your legs to manage pressure at the end of a turn. Let the pressure that builds on your skis cause your legs to bend.

(c) To make the transition between turns, explore changing edges sooner, before the end of turn completion. With early edge action, you can move swiftly out of a turn, and not turn more than necessary.

(d) Be strong in your upper body—across your chest and down your arms, holding your pole grips firmly.

(e) Increase your ankle flex slightly and slightly change your edge angle to make adjustments in your turn.

(f) Work toward the sensation of the upper body moving down the hill with the lower body moving from side to side. Imagine a straight line down the hill. While carving turns, keep your upper body centered above the line and see how far you can get your skis away from the line. Your upper body should stay at the same height off the snow throughout the run.

BEND AND EXTEND TURNS. Practice an exercise called, *Bend and Extend*. It provides a helpful exaggeration of the movement pattern of dynamic carved turns. (FIGURE 8.25)

Figure 8.25

Bend deeply and change edges.

Through the completion of a turn, bend your legs deeper than usual, to a squat position. As your body moves down the hill, tip and turn onto opposite edges and extend your legs quickly against the skis. Attempt to extend in a lateral direction (down the hill) and not purely upward. As you extend your legs, the pressure that bends your skis into an arc will increase (FIGURE 8.26). Keep your feet apart to allow for edging and your weight forward to compensate for the low position. Aim your upper body down the hill.

DYNAMIC RETRACTION TURN. In a carved turn, your body inclines toward the center of the turn. The lower body is extended to the inside and the upper body is relatively vertical in a hip-angulated and countered position. You can achieve this position early in a turn by extending your legs against an edged ski (see *Dynamic Carved Turns*). Alternatively, you can achieve this position *very*

FIGURE 8.26
Extend against the edged ski.

early in the turn by a retraction technique.

Retraction refers to pulling the legs upward, under the body, very rapidly. In a retraction motion, you pull your feet up so quickly that you are momentarily unweighted. This action of retracting your legs occurs at the transition between turns. When retraction occurs, the skis are very light on the snow or come off the snow entirely. At this moment, the legs are extended quickly to the outside of the upcoming turn, and the skis are tipped onto opposite edges. As the skier falls back to the snow, his/her body weight, plus the force of breaking the fall, is transmitted to the edged ski, bending it into a tight arc.

A dynamic retraction turn requires sufficient speed to pressure the skis into a deep arc prior to the transition to the upcoming turn. The momentary lift of the legs is aided by the upward spring of the skis when the pressure is relieved. The energy previously stored in the bent skis helps speed the upward (unweighting) motion of the feet.

An additional change of direction of the path can be achieved by pivoting the skis when they are unweighted, and/or by steering the skis as they touch down. Thereafter, pressure on the edged skis controls the carved turn.

PULL FEET BACK. As you lower your body by flexing at the end of a turn, it is natural for weight to move behind the balance point of your foot. It is important to adjust your weight forward again, over the ball of your foot, to start the next turn accurately. Traditionally, the body is levered forward from the ankle to seek the balance point. Instead, this position can be attained by pulling the feet back under the body, at the instant the skis are unweighted during retraction. This is an efficient movement that is done simultaneously with extending the legs sideways and tipping the skis on edge.

In the adjoining photographs, the skier's weight is adjusted by pulling the feet back (FIGURE 8.27 and FIGURE 8.28). The Slalom pole provides a vertical reference to help recognize the change of body position. Although this exercise is performed on weighted skis, you can gain experience by practicing the movement from a standing position. Use your ski poles for support as you pull your

FIGURE 8.27

*The skier's center of mass is behind
the ball of the foot.*

FIGURE 8.28

*The feet have been pulled back to
align the skier's center of mass
over the ball of the foot.*

feet back.

DYNAMIC SHORT RADIUS TURNS. The design of deep side-cut skis makes it possible to link carved turns of relatively short radii (FIGURE 8.29). Some steering (an additional torque that is applied by the leg), will be necessary during the turn to tighten the arc more than sidecut allows. Steering should be kept to a minimum to reduce skidding. Pursue carving whenever possible.

Begin with a carved turn on gentle terrain. Increase the edge angle to scribe a smaller arc. Aim your upper body down the hill and use lower body movements, only. Move quickly from one set

of edges to the other, increasing the pace of the turns.

For dynamic short radius turns on steeper terrain, use the retraction movements described earlier. As you extend your legs laterally to meet the snow, pull your feet back and tip your skis on edge. On very steep terrain, it is necessary to control speed by reducing the proportion of the time the skis are pointing downhill. During the unweighted phase of retraction, pivot the skis away from the fall line and then proceed with a tight carved turn.

As you work on short radius turns, practice the following:

(a) Edge and pressure your skis at the beginning of an arc, before steering your feet.

(b) To start a turn, begin in a low stance and extend your skis outwards, away from the center of the turn.

(c) Start with a medium radius turn and tighten the turn radius progressively.

(d) Alternate quick turns with medium radius turns.

(e) Perform quick turns on one ski.

(f) Contrast elegant medium radius turns (tall stance, feet together) with short radius turns (lower stance, feet apart).

FIGURE 8.29

With feet apart, tip both feet/skis in the same direction onto edges to begin a turn. Aim the upper body at a point down the hill as your lower body moves actively.

Deep Sidecut Carve

FIGURE 8.30

Start in an arc moving backward and finish in an arc moving forward.

REVERSE 180 TURN. The *Reverse 180 Turn* is an exercise that links turns in a different pattern than usual (FIGURE 8.30). In this maneuver, you move in both forward and backward directions. It provides a fun and challenging way to sharpen edging skills and play with pressure along the length of the ski. The *Reverse 180 Turn* should be performed on a very smooth slope of moderate pitch.

Start with your ski tips pointing slightly uphill and your head and body turned to look downhill. Slide backward on uphill edges. Shift your weight toward the tails of your skis. They will act very much like the ski tips and your skis will carve a smooth arc away from the fall line as you travel backwards. Continue to turn, without stepping, until your skis point down the hill. Change to opposite edges, lever forward to the tips, and scribe a forward arc through the fall line and continuing in the arc until your skis point diagonally up the hill. As your speed stalls, change edges, lever

FIGURE 8.31

In this more difficult variation of the 180 turn, the maneuver is started in a forward direction.

back and slide backward, repeating the exercise. Throughout the maneuver, twist your upper body as much as possible to face in, or close to, the downhill direction.

With practice, this exercise can be performed down the length of a long pitch, smoothly and rhythmically. Then, try a 180 turn starting in a forward direction (FIGURE 8.31).

MEDLEY. Have fun with different turn variations. With practice, you will become a more versatile skier and better able to adapt to different terrain and snow condition. Here are some options to consider:

    (a) vary speed from very slow to very fast

    (b) vary turn radius from short to medium to long

    (c) alternate a specific number of short turns with a specific number of long turns

    (d) change edges quickly for short, tight arcs

    (e) change edges slowly for long, drawn-out arcs

    (f) vary the width of your stance from narrow to overly wide

    (g) ski diagonally down a hill instead of turning in the fall line ❄

S elect the exercises or subjects from each category that you would like to practice. Refer back to this outline to change your lesson plan for subsequent days.

LESSON PLAN

WARM YOUR BODY. Refer to Chapter 9, *On the Snow Warmup* for suggestions of exercises to warm and stretch your body.

RHYTHM AND REVIEW. On smooth, gentle terrain, begin with edging movements, tipping skis from one set of edges to the other. Make sure your feet are apart. Be patient and let the edge engagement scribe an arc that tightens naturally as you cross the fall line. Take care to stay over the balance point (ball of foot) in order for the ski to work optimally. Encourage a countered position with a deliberate lead of the inside ski (lead ski).

  (a) stand over the balance point
  (b) feet apart with both skis on the snow
  (c) inside ski lead begins early in the turn
  (d) edge change at the very start of the turn
  (e) the inside edge of the outside ski gripping throughout the turn
  (f) Maximizing Speed (*Perceptual Skills*, Chapter 10)

DIRECTED FREE SKIING. Start on smooth, moderate terrain where you can feel very comfortable with the execution of the turn. This will allow you to focus your attention on the sensations derived from your actions. Feel the "G-force" that builds in a carved turn, particularly as the radius of the turn tightens. Feel the deliberate feeling of the inside edge of the foot/ski cutting through the snow.

SCHOOLWORK. Review the description and photographs that coincide with the titles you choose.

  (a) *Traverse Using Sidecut*
  (b) *Traverse Exercises*
  (c) *Turn Completion*
  (d) *Edge Change*
  (e) *Link Carved Turns*
  (f) *Diagonal Descent*
  (g) *Round Arc*
  (h) *Increase Speed*
  (i) *Dynamic Carved Turns*
  (j) *Bend and Extend Turns*
  (k) *Dynamic Retraction Turn*
  (l) *Pull Feet Back*
  (m) *Dynamic Short Radius Turns*
  (n) *Reverse 180 Turn*
  (o) *Medley*

MOUNTAIN PLAYGROUND. Play with how far you can reach

your skis out to the side and still have them come back underneath you.

SLOW AND EASY. Back off on intensity and "ride the edge" on moderate terrain.

LESSON PLAN EXAMPLE:

WARM YOUR BODY.
    (a) *Jumping Jacks*
    (b) *Knee Lift*
    (c) *Knee to Elbow*
    (d) *Head Lean*
    (e) *Arm Circle Variation*
    (f) *Hip Circles*
    (g) *Side Stretch*
    (h) *Twisting Movements*
    (i) *Calf Stretch*
    (j) *Inside Leg Stretch*
    (k) *Tail Stretch*
    (l) *Tip Stretch*

RHYTHM AND REVIEW.
    (a) inside ski lead begins early in the turn
    (b) edge change at the very start of the turn

DIRECTED FREE SKIING. On smooth, moderate terrain, ski fast through slow turns. (See *Maximizing Speed*, Chapter 10, *Perceptual Skills*.) Feel the "G-force" that builds in a carved turn, particularly as the radius of the turn tightens. Feel the deliberate feeling of the inside edge of the foot/ski cutting through the snow. Explore these sensations as you vary the size of your turn and the intensity of your movements.

SCHOOLWORK.

Deep Sidecut Carve

(a) *Traverse Using Sidecut*
(b) *Traverse Exercises*
(c) *Turn Completion*
(d) *Edge Change*

MOUNTAIN PLAYGROUND. Ski on slopes in which the pitch changes. Experiment with the amount you can "reach" your skis out to the side at the start of the turn.

SLOW AND EASY. Back off on intensity and "ride the edge" on moderate terrain. ❄

Soaring

CHAPTER 9:
ON THE SNOW WARM-UP

Described and pictured on the following pages are exercises you can use to start your day or to get warm on cold days.

Have you ever noticed that the farther away you are from a warming lodge, the colder and stiffer you become? To avoid injury, it is important to warm the body (raise the body temperature) and then stretch the muscles and joints. Warm-up and stretching exercises follow. The warm-up exercises also contribute to cardiovascular fitness.

Perform all warm-up and stretching exercises on flat terrain. ❄

WARM-UP EXERCISES

RUN IN PLACE. Lift your knees to run in place. Use your ski poles for balance and support.

KNEE LIFT. Repeatedly lift one knee and then the other. Begin with small lifts and increase the height of the lifted ski gradually. Use your ski poles for balance (FIGURE 9.1).

FIGURE 9.1

The weight of the ski equipment increases the amount of effort expended in this exercise.

SIDE STEP OVER POLES. Place one ski pole on the snow. Stand beside the pole. Then, step over the pole with the ski that is closest to the pole. Touch the ski on the snow momentarily before bringing it back to its original place. Cross this ski back and forth over the pole before repeating the exercise with the other ski (FIGURE 9.2).

FIGURE 9.2

This exercise is also helpful for practicing the transfer of weight from one ski to the other.

ONE SKI SCOOTER. With one ski removed, push off with your ski boot and glide on the ski (FIGURE 9.3). Scooter to a distant object on flat terrain. Scooter around objects such as ski poles, cones, or Slalom poles.

FIGURE 9.3

Drive your hands forward as you push off with your foot to help maintain balance over the support leg.

JUMP IN PLACE. Jump in place lifting your ski tails, your ski tips and your whole ski (FIGURE 9.4) off the snow.

JUMPING JACKS. Alternate jumping with feet together and apart. Touch your arms to your sides when your feet are together. Touch your arms overhead when your feet are apart. For a variation, move your arms forward and backward while you maintain jumping jack leg movements. Also try circling your arms with one arm moving forward and the other arm moving backward.

FIGURE 9.4

Push down on your ski poles as you jump with your legs.

KNEE TO ELBOW. Without using ski poles, stand with your hands clasped behind your head. Lift one knee to touch the opposite elbow (FIGURE 9.5). Before trying this exercise with skis, practice it without skis. Alternate sides.

FIGURE 9.5

Keep your back fairly upright and twist your upper body to touch your knee.

Racer, Chuck Ginsberg

FIGURE 9.6 (left)
Body position in a low tuck.

FIGURE 9.7 (right)
From a low tuck position, extend your legs to obtain a high tuck.

DOWNHILL RACER. In a stationary position on flat terrain, "ski" an imaginary downhill course. The course can include elements such as a:

    (a) low tuck out of the start (FIGURE 9.6)

    (b) high tuck over bumps (FIGURE 9.7)

    (c) turns in a high tuck

    (d) long turns in a low tuck

    (e) press over a roll

    (f) stand through the finish ❄

STRETCHING EXERCISES

Before stretching your muscles, it is very important to warm-up with aerobic exercise. Then, stretch slowly, until you feel the stretch. Hold the stretched position for at least 30 seconds. To avoid injury, do not force the stretch. Repeat each stretch, holding the position. Stretch both sides of the body when applicable.

HEAD MOVEMENT. Move your head forward and back to warm up your neck muscles. As you bend your head forward, touch your chin to your chest. As you bring your head back, lift your chin and keep your shoulders down. Also, turn your head to the side and look as far as you can over your shoulder.

HEAD LEAN. Stretch the side of your neck by leaning your head toward your shoulder. Keep your shoulders down (FIGURE 9.8).

FIGURE 9.8
Tilt your ear toward your shoulder.

FIGURES 9.9 a and 9.9 b
Vary the size and speed of your arm circles.

ARM CIRCLES. With straight arms, circle your arms forward and backward to warm your shoulder muscles (FIGURE 9.9 a and b).

FIGURE 9.10 a, b, c
One arm circles in a forward direction while the other arm circles in the opposite direction.

ARM CIRCLE VARIATION. Start with straight arms over your head. Then, circle one arm forward and the other arm backward (FIGURE 9.10 a, b, c). Both arms should be at your sides and overhead at the same time during the circling movement. Change directions.

ARM ROUTINE. Keep your arms at shoulder height as you repeat this routine: elbows back, arms back, cross arms FIGURES 9.11 a, b, c).

FIGURE 9.11
*Elbows back (left),
arms back (middle),
arms crossed (right)*

HIP CIRCLES. Stand with your feet apart and your hands on your hips. Move your hips in a circle as you keep your head in the same place. Start with a small circle and increase the size gradually.

SIDE STRETCH. Stretch to the side without bending forward at the waist (FIGURE 9.12).

FIGURE 9.12
*Hold a ski pole between your hands
and pull gently with the lower hand
to increase the stretch.*

FIGURE 9.13

Lift your upper arm and press it toward your back. Cross your lower hand past the opposite leg.

TWISTING MOVEMENTS. Following are three different twisting exercises:

(a) Twist your upper body to look behind you. Hold your arms out to the side at shoulder level.

(b) Stand with your feet apart. Bend forward at the waist and swing your arms from side-to-side, twisting your upper body (Figure 9.13).

(c) Stand with both arms stretched overhead. Hold the ends of a ski pole between your hands. Twist the pole to turn your body until you feel the stretch through your torso. Twist in both directions.

CALF STRETCH. Slide one ski forward to stretch the back of the other leg (9.14). Keep your upper body upright and use your poles for balance. Since your ski boot holds your heel down, the stretch to the calf muscle is intensified.

FIGURE 9.14

Take a giant step forward to stretch the back of your leg

INSIDE LEG STRETCH. Bend one knee toward the ski tip and extend the other leg to stretch the inside of your straight leg (FIGURE 9.15 and FIGURE 9.16).

FIGURE 9.15 (left)
Stretch the muscles along the inside of your extended leg.

FIGURE 9.16 (right)
Slide the outstretched leg forward and back (pictured) to increase the stretch.

TAIL STRETCH. Using your ski poles for support and balance, place the tail of one ski in the snow near the other ski tip. Stretch the back of your lifted leg (FIGURE 9.17). Bend forward to increase the stretch.

FIGURE 9.17 (left)
Slide the support ski back slightly to increase the stretch.

FIGURE 9.18 (right)
Increase the bend of the support leg to increase the stretch.

TIP STRETCH. Using your ski poles for support and balance, place the tip of one ski in the snow behind the tail of the other ski. Bend the support leg and slide it forward as you keep your upper body upright (FIGURE 9.18). You should feel the stretch in the thigh of your lifted leg. ❄

Mountain playground

Photo: Dobber Price

CHAPTER 10:
PERCEPTUAL SKILLS

Sights, sounds, and tactile sensations all provide essential cues about terrain, snow conditions, speed, and distances. Developing perceptual skills involves observing and using these cues effectively (FIGURE 10.1).

Perceptual refers to any awareness that is acquired directly through the senses. You can develop the ability to process sensory information and use it instantly to actuate precise physical movements. This is an important aspect of ski performance that is often overlooked.

The majority of the following exercises enhance visual skills. It is important to develop visual awareness to judge speeds and distances and to use imagery effectively. ❊

VISUAL PERCEPTION

NOTICE OBJECTS. Visual awareness is necessary to avoid other skiers and potentially dangerous objects. Look ahead to survey your surroundings.

To notice more distant objects, practice by looking for objects on the hill, such as signs, blue jackets, lift tower pads, etc. Count the objects to enforce the discipline of observing them.

READ TERRAIN. To use visual cues effectively requires concentration, practice and experience. To prepare for and adapt to terrain changes, notice and "read" the terrain.

FIGURE 10.1

It is necessary to use visual, tactile and auditory perceptions in order to stay synchronized.

FIGURE 10.2
Look ahead to determine your line through bumps.

Immediately after you ski a run, try to describe the terrain. Identify pitch, transitions from flat to steep or steep to flat slopes, uneven surfaces, side hills, rolls and bumps. Does the trail wind down the mountain, turning to the left or right? Ski the run a second time and verbally describe the terrain as you descend.

LOOK AHEAD. In order to negotiate terrain changes or varying snow conditions smoothly, it is important to look ahead (FIGURE 10.2).

Play follow-the-leader to encourage looking ahead. The leader must look down the hill to choose a smooth, interesting, or exciting path. He or she determines the size, shape, and speed of the turns. The follower stays in the leader's tracks by focusing on the path of the leader's skis, or by watching the leader's body movements.

IMAGERY. In skiing, imagery is most often used to form a mental picture that closely resembles an action. For example, *imagine* skiing precise and technically correct turns. It is important to imagine the feel, the sound and the appearance of excellent form, instead of merely observing other skiers as a spectator.

Visualize skiing a run that you know well. Decide what turns to make in order to control or maintain speed where the pitch of the slope changes.

Imagine setting a course to include rhythm changes which correspond to changes in terrain. Where on the hill should rounder turns be set to control speed? Where should gates be set closer to the fall line to let skis run? How should gates be set to bring the course across the hill?

Imagery can be used to provide an analogy, such as to compare balancing on the edge of a ski to balancing on a tight rope. Another example is envisioning a crayon underfoot that leaves circular arcs on the snow. ❊

TACTILE AND VISUAL PERCEPTION

JUDGING SPEED. It is important to have a sense of how fast you are moving as well as the time and distance needed to slow down. Awareness of speed depends greatly upon the sense of touch. Sharper perceptions of tactile sensations means greater sensitivity to the relationships between speed, turn size and centrifugal force.

Set up tasks ahead of time, such as stopping at a given point on the hill, or stopping on a given turn—such as the tenth turn. These tasks require the ability to judge and adjust speed of descent.

REGULATING SPEED. Find a skier who is moving at a consistent speed down the hill. Slow down to move farther away, or speed up to get closer to that skier. Be aware of how you regulate your speed. To slow down, experiment with sharper turns, more turn completion, or skidded turns. To increase speed, choose a shallower turn arc, less turn completion, and minimize skidding.

JUDGING DISTANCE. Judging speed plays an important role in judging distances. The ability to judge both enables skiers to adapt to different terrain features and racers to choose the best line in a race course (FIGURE 10.3).

To learn to judge distances better, decide how many turns it will take to ski from one point on the hill to another point that is farther away. Ski the designated number of turns and see if you finish at the second point. Then, fill the same distance with a different number of turns of another radius.

MAXIMIZING SPEED. On easy terrain, at a slow speed, ski as cleanly as possible through the arc of each turn, maximizing the speed for the situation. When the ski travels forward through the arc of the turn, it will carry more speed than if it skids sideways. In other words, ski fast through slow turns. Continue this theme for higher speed turns.

FIGURE 10.3

A racer must process sensory information and use it instantly to actuate precise physical movements.

Ski racer, Onie Bolduc

FREE-SKI/COURSE. This drill is excellent for developing perceptual skills since you must rely on visual input to judge the speed, size, and shape of turns in relation to distance down the hill (FIGURE 10.4).

Set short courses of four to six Slalom poles or cones at intervals down a long run. Ski the whole run moving smoothly from the course into free-skiing and back into the course. Look ahead to match the radius of the turns in the upcoming course. ❄

AUDITORY PERCEPTION

VERBAL CUES. Talking to yourself can help emphasize an action. For example, saying "up, down" can promote movement, "left, right" can focus attention on the outside ski, and "turn, turn" can help develop a rhythm.

LISTEN TO SKI SOUNDS. As well as being important for skiing safely, sensitivity to sound can help refine timing, weight transfer, and rhythm. It can encourage awareness of edge action and help improve carving.

Listen to the sound that your skis make on a hard snow surface. Notice the louder sound when your skis skid sideways and the quieter sound when your skis carve through the arc of a turn. Work toward keeping your skis quiet on the snow. ❄

FIGURE 10.4

Ski to and from short courses that are spaced at intervals along a slope.

Skier, David Lamb

The Mountain Playground

New snow had fallen the night before. My group gathered around me before the mountain was awakened by crowds of powder seekers. In the early morning light, eager eyes shined through goggles on faces hidden under hats and zipped-up collars. Greetings were whispered or nodded, no one daring to disturb the quiet morning and break the spell of anticipation.

"Let's go to the playground!" spoke a little voice belonging to Brett, the youngest of the group. "You know," he continued, "the place off the side of the Meadows. My mountain playground."

The slope he referred to fell away from the edge of the Meadows, gradually disappearing into the woods below. A fire had claimed much of the hillside but had left fallen logs amongst tree stumps and boulders. On this day, the regrowth of small pine trees was covered with new snow and only the shapes of the obstructions were visible. The wind had blown the night before, sculpting the snow into a white world of snow drifts, rolls, ridges, dips and jumps.

The deep snow muffled the sounds of skiing as we approached the Meadows. I remember how the silence burst into laughter and shouts of delight as Brett led the way into the playground. From the Meadow's edge, I viewed the mountain from a new perspective.

New snow had fallen the night before on another occasion: Members of the PSIA Demonstration Team gathered around their coach in anticipation of skiing for a film. As a team member, I spoke of the mountain in the way that Brett had enlightened me. From my comments, the film became entitled, "The Mountain Playground." It emphasized the application of technique to the challenges of the terrain, of the mountain.

This led to national focus, and the theme was introduced internationally at Interski in 1987. The presentation by the Professional Ski Instructors of America began with, "The purpose of our workshop is to demonstrate how the student's enjoyment of the mountain playground is enhanced by developing new movement possibilities and strategies." All because of the words spoken by a six-year-old on a wintry day. ✳

GLOSSARY

Aerodynamic: describes the position a skier assumes in order to cut through the air with the least amount of air resistance.

Angulation: bending sideways to maximize balance on an edged ski. Angulation can occur in the knees and hips (in combination with flexing of these joints) and the spinal column.

Arc: the curved path of the ski in the snow.

Balance point: the balance point is located at the middle of the sole of the foot on traditional and deep sidecut skis. This point corresponds to the most efficient location to apply downward force to a ski. Skis are designed to bend into a circular arc when forces are applied at the balance point. Subtle fore and aft movements originate from this point.

Balanced stance: the way the parts of the body are aligned to stay in balance. Constant muscular adjustments are necessary to maintain balance. A balanced stance is the optimum position from which a skier can move effectively and efficiently. In a balanced position, the skier's center of mass (weight) is over the feet.

Banking: leaning inward (inclining toward the inside of the turn) with a relatively straight body position.

Bevel: refers to the angle at which the metal edge of the ski slants. The side and bottom of the edge are beveled to create a sharper edge angle than ninety degrees.

Carving: weighting and angulating the ski so that it bends into a circular arc, whereby the edge of the ski moves along a corresponding circular arc to form a sharp curved track in the snow. In pure carving, every point along the length of the ski follows the same path along the arc of the turn and there is no skidding.

Centrifugal: away from a center. A skier is pulled to the outside of a turn by centrifugal force.

Chatter: the edge of the ski catches in the snow and bounces repeatedly to a lower path. Chatter can occur when the edge of the ski is at too steep of an angle.

Countered position: the outside hip is slightly back in relation to the inside hip in a turn. The downhill hip is slightly back in relation to the uphill hip in a traverse. Countering movements generally occur with angulation of the hip and spine.

Cross-over transition: the skier's body crosses over the skis during the transition between turns.

Cross-under transition: the skier's legs quickly move laterally under the body during the transition between turns.

Crud snow: snow that is inconsistent in depth and density.

Curvilinear: describing a line or path that curves.

Directed free skiing: focus of attention on specific technical or tactical elements while free skiing.

Dynamic: refers to the rapid adjustments of body position that the skier makes to stay in balance.

Edge angle: the amount a ski is tipped on edge. The edge angle is measured relative to a horizontal surface.

Edging: tipping of the ski onto one of its edges.

Fall line: through any point on the hill, the fall line is the direction where the hill has the steepest slope. A snowball will roll in that direction.

Garland: incomplete turn that results in diagonal travel down a hill. Garland turns provide an effective exercise for practicing the entry or completion phase of a turn repeatedly.

Gliding: carved turns in which skiers maximize speed by using the least amount of edge angle necessary to maintain their intended direction of travel.

Hip angulation: an angle at the hip between the upper body and lower body. The upper body stays relatively vertical, with shoulders relatively level, while the lower body is at a slant to the snow. This is a strong position because the skeletal alignment from the foot to the hip provides support.

Inside ski: considering that a turn is part of a circle, the inside ski is closer to the center of the circle.

Javelin: an exercise in which the skier balances on the outside ski of the turn while the inside ski is lifted across the front of the outside ski. The placement of the inside ski encourages a countered position and makes it very difficult to rotate the outside hip through the turn.

Lead ski: inside ski of a turn, having a forward movement, or *lead*, in relation to the position of the outside ski.

Line: the skier's path down a slope. It is often referred to in a bump run or a race course.

Linked turns: the completion of one turn leads directly into the start of the next turn.

Open stance: the skis are apart in a position that is comfortable and stable.

Outside ski: considering that a turn is part of a circle, the outside ski is farther from the center of the circle.

Over-edging: using more edge than is necessary for a given situation.

Parallel position: the center line of the skis are at an equal distance apart for their whole length. The tips point straight ahead and not toward or away from each other.

Pivoting: twisting of a flat ski by rotating the foot about an axis perpendicular to the surface of the snow. The skier's direction of travel does not change.

Pressure: pressure of the ski against the snow is that part of the total force that acts upon each square inch of the contact surface. Since pressure is not uniform along the length and width of the ski, the term usually refers to how the total force is distributed along the length of the ski.

Pressure control: adjustments a skier makes to control the location of the center of force acting on the skis. Weight transfer from ski to ski, fore/aft movements, and flexing/extending actions affect the amount and location of pressure on a ski.

Radius: distance from the center of a circle to the edge of the circle. Tight turns in which the center of the turn is close to the track of the ski are referred to as short radius turns. When the distance between the turn center and ski track is great, turns are considered to be long radius turns. In racing, Slalom turns are generally classified as short radius turns. Giant Slalom turns are medium radius, and Super-G and Downhill turns are long radius turns.

Railed ski: an insufficiently weighted and over-edged ski that tracks forward. Typically, a skier's intention is to turn when railing occurs.

Rebound: the springing back, or recoiling of a ski that has been bent in reverse camber.

Reverse Camber: camber is the bend in a ski that is apparent when the bases of two skis are placed together. Camber distributes the weight of a skier along the running surface of a ski. Reverse camber occurs when the camber is pressed flat and the ski bows in the other direction. This happens when a ski is bent in an arc during a turn.

Rhythmic turns: a series of turns of the same radius and speed.

Rotary action: the action of turning or twisting the body along its vertical axis.

Rotary leg movements: the turning or twisting movement of the legs beneath a stable upper body.

Sidecut: the difference in width of a ski at its tip, tail and middle. Skis are wider at the tip and tail in comparison to the middle of the ski. In general, the more side-cut a ski has, the sharper it will turn.

Sidecut radius: the measurement of the tightest radius of which a ski of a particular length will carve a turn.

Side hill: the slope falls away from the skier's direction of travel.

Skidding: sideways travel on an angulated ski that changes the skier's direction. In a skidded turn, a pivot of an insufficiently angulated ski occurs.

Sliding: forward travel of a flat ski.

Slipping: sideways travel of a flat ski.

Square position: the skier's body faces in the same direction as the skis point.

Steering: an additional torque that is applied to change the path of the ski from the path of pure carving. The torque causes a pivoting action, such that steering always adds a skidding motion to the ski. Steering is applied to decrease the radius of an otherwise pure carved turn.

Stem: a stepping movement in which the lifted ski is placed at an angle to the other ski. The angle is such that the ski tips are close and the tails are apart.

Straight run: when a skier slides straight down a slope while standing in a balanced position with weight distributed equally on both skis.

Synchronize: two or more skiers start and finish turns at the same time. Skiers can be in a horizontal, vertical or diagonal formation, or no fixed formation.

Tactics: how a skier applies his/her technique to a skiing situation. A skier's strategy: where to turn, at what speed and the kind of turn that will be used.

Technique: how the formal elements of skiing are performed. Technique is usually evaluated by comparison with optimum body positions and ski positions for every type of maneuver encountered in free-skiing or racing. Optimum technique is a constantly evolving standard, subject to the current judgment of coaches, racers and skiing authorities.

Traverse: gliding across a hill in a parallel ski relationship on uphill edges.

Trough: carved out channels between bumps.

Tuck: a compact, aerodynamic body position in which the back of the skier is essentially parallel to the surface of the skis.

Under-edging: using less edge than is necessary for a given situation. ❊

T he following corrective plan will help you take an active role toward self improvement. Also, it is helpful to take a lesson and have a professional assess your progress. In this way, you will be sure that your performance and your perception of your performance are the same.

In the following, incorrect actions are described, negative outcomes are identified, and a plan for improvement is given. Often in the lesson plan, a reference will be made to an exercise within the book. A page number will follow each title to help you find the exercise quickly. The same exercise may be used in more than one way.

APPENDIX I
CORRECTING ERRORS

COMMON ERRORS. You may have become aware of difficulties that occur during a part of a turn, or you may have been told that a position or movement is not quite right. Scan the following list of common errors to identify a position or action that may cause problems in your skiing.

(a) Leaning Back
(b) Bending Forward
(c) Narrow Stance
(d) Arm Position
(e) Pole Swing
(f) Looking Down
(g) Stiff Outside Leg
(h) Upper Body Rotation
(i) Banking (leaning of the upper body)
(j) Excessive Weight on the Inside Ski
(k) Inside Ski Lift
(l) Railing

LEANING BACK. Some skiers tend to sit or lean back against the back of their boots. This causes body weight to fall behind the balance point of the foot (mid-foot for traditional skis, ball of foot for deep sidecut skis). A rearward position requires strength and can become tiresome quickly. Also, from this position, it is difficult to edge the ski at the start of a turn or apply sufficient tip pressure to enact a carve. At the completion of a turn, rearward lean decreases edge angle and causes skidding. Indications of leaning back are:

(a) tired thighs
(b) crossed ski tips
(c) skidded turns
(d) lack of control on steep terrain
(e) skis "run away"
(f) arms that are back
(g) arms that are too high

Lesson Plan:

1. *Balance Point*, page 53. When you lean back, your weight is concentrated behind the balance point under the sole of your foot.
2. Maintain contact between the lower leg and the front of the boot.
3. Ski on gentle terrain.
4. *Lift the Inside Ski*, page 97. Lift the tail of the inside ski.
5. Practice *Bobbing*, page 98, to maintain contact or increase pressure against the front of the boot.

BENDING FORWARD. Bending forward at the hips restricts leg and spine movements and the ability to absorb uneven terrain fully and smoothly. It also inhibits angulation and countering movements. Indications of bending forward are:

(a) a straight or arched back
(b) chin lifted to compensate for forward lean
(c) sticking the buttocks out
(d) stiff legs
(e) arms that are too low

Lesson Plan:

1. *Body Position*, page 52, provides a description of proper body position.
2. *Practice the Stance*, page 53, provides exercises to assess your stance and make corrections.
3. Practice a pelvic tilt position to round the lower back. Lie down on your back with your knees bent and press the small

of your back against the floor. Retain this body alignment when you stand. This is the basic stance position.

4. With proper body position, practice a traverse, stepping from foot to foot, lifting your knees.

NARROW STANCE. Balance is difficult with a stance that is too narrow. In a narrow stance, the inside leg inhibits the inward lean of the outside leg as the edge angle increases. A wider stance allows room to tip the outside ski onto a steep angle.

Since the tips and tails of deep sidecut skis are considerably wider than traditional skis, it is natural that skiers place their feet further apart (feet approximately hip width apart). Indications of a narrow stance are:

(a) skis that are close or touching
(b) "catching" edges
(c) exaggerated hip movement
(d) skidded turns

Lesson Plan:

1. Compare a narrow position with a wide stance while sliding straight down a nearly flat slope.
2. Practice traverses using a wide stance. In a traverse on a steep slope, the uphill ski lead and counter position will be greater than on a relatively flatter slope.
3. Experiment with an overly wide stance and then return to a normal (wide) stance.

ARM POSITION. Holding your arms in an improper position can upset balance and cause fatigue. Arms should be in a relaxed position and shoulders should not be raised. Extraneous arm movements can be a result of other incorrect actions. Or, arm movements can be the cause of a problem. Indications of improper arm positions and their resultant outcomes are:

(a) Arms that are held too high lessen stability and cause weight to move behind the balance point.
(b) Arms that are held too low encourage a forward bend at the waist.

(c) Arms that are back cause weight to move back.

(d) Arm separation that is too narrow inhibits lateral angulation and a countered position.

(e) Arms that are spread too wide inhibit pole swing and cause body rotation.

(f) An outside arm that is too high causes leaning (banking) toward the center of the turn.

(g) An inside arm that is too low also causes leaning (banking) toward the center of the turn.

(h) Arms that cross in front of the body cause rotation of the upper body, which can cause skidding.

Lesson Plan:

1. To find an effective arm position, shrug your shoulders up to your ears. Pretend you have lead weights in your hands that pull your hands (and shoulders) down. Then, lift your hands in front for balance. Your hands should be several inches wider apart than the width of your body. Hold poles with a firm, yet not tense, grip. Point the ski pole tips behind you.

2. Ski without poles. Clap your hands, moving them no farther apart than described previously. This exercise is helpful for keeping your arms in front of your body.

3. *Horizontal Pole*, page 137. Place your hands at the appropriate distance apart.

4. *Arm Position*, page 148. This is an exercise that uses surveyor's ribbon to effect arm position.

5. *Arms Crossed*, page 136. Use this exercise to assess and improve your performance.

POLE ACTION. Excessive arm movement is detrimental to an effective pole plant. The pole plant should not disrupt the flow of movement in a turn. Indications of incorrect pole action are:

(a) improper timing of pole plants (too early or too late)

(b) dropping the inside hand or lifting the outside hand

(c) hands positioned too high or too low

(d) planting out to the side

(e) crossing an arm in front of the body

(f) forward movement of the shoulder

(g) leaving the pole in the snow too long

(h) relying on dragging the poles for balance

(i) gripping the pole too tightly or too loosely

Lesson Plan:

1. *Pole Straps*, page 78. Check that you are using the strap on the grip properly.

2. *Pole Swing*, page 100. Practice a correct pole swing.

3. *Timing of the Pole Action*, page 100. Examine the timing of your pole plant.

4. *Touch/Plant*, page 100. Examine the force of your pole plant.

5. Ski a consistent turn radius on smooth terrain as you practice your pole plant.

LOOKING DOWN. When you look down you see the area immediately in front of your skis. It is important to look farther down the hill to prepare for changes in terrain or snow conditions, or avoid people and obstacles. Looking down decreases effective peripheral vision and overall balance. Indications of looking down are:

(a) chin down

(b) seeing the tips of your skis

(c) late reactions to changes in terrain and snow conditions

(d) having to lift your head to look ahead

Lesson Plan:

1. *Notice Objects*, page 222. Look ahead to find specific objects.

2. *Read Terrain*, page 222. Notice and remember terrain features.

3. *Look Ahead*, page 223. Follow-the-leader to encourage looking ahead.

4. *Free Ski/Course*, page 226. A drill with Slalom poles or cones that encourages looking ahead, judging distance and judging speed.

5. Use a verbal reminder, such as, "look" as you ski increasingly more difficult terrain.

STIFF OUTSIDE LEG. A stiff outside leg does not allow you to absorb terrain changes smoothly or manage the forces that develop through a turn. It is difficult to increase edge angle and continue a turn when legs are stiff. Therefore, skidded turns result.

Indications of a stiff outside leg:

    (a) skidded turns, edge does not hold

    (b) inside ski supports more weight than is necessary

    (c) arcs are not smooth or round

    (d) it is difficult to complete one turn and start the next turn

    (e) it is difficult to ski varied terrain, particularly moguls

    (f) it is difficult to ski powder or crud conditions

Lesson Plan:

1. Focus on flexing the ankle and increasing pressure against the front of the boot.
2. *Bobbing*, page 98, an exercise that encourages flexing and extending actions of the legs.
3. *Leaping*, page 97, an exercise that requires downward movement in order to spring off the snow.
4. *Lift Inside Ski*, page 97. It is necessary to bend the outside leg to perform this exercise successfully.

UPPER BODY ROTATION. Rotary action is the action of turning or twisting the body along its vertical axis. When the upper body starts into a turn first, upper body rotation occurs. The force applied by rotating the upper body in the direction of the turn causes the legs to rotate and skidding to result. Indications of upper body rotation are:

    (a) skidded turns

    (b) turning with the hips

    (c) "square" vs., countered body position

    (d) not facing the upcoming turn

    (e) crossing the outside arm in front of the body

Lesson Plan:

1. Traverse in a javelin position with the front of the uphill ski crossed over the front of the downhill ski. A countered (and not rotated) body position occurs. Retain this position as

you return to a parallel stance.

2. *Javelin Turns*, page 117. The placement of the inside ski in a javelin turn makes it very difficult to rotate the outside hip through the turn.

3. *Inside Ski Lead*, page 188. Early ski lead coincides with a countered body position at the start of a turn.

4. *Horizontal Pole*, page 137. Turning the pole toward the center of the turn indicates upper body rotation.

5. *Target Skiing*, page 134. Direct your upper body at a point down the hill and turn your legs only.

6. *Hop Turns*, page 138. Hop turns develop strong lower body rotary movements of the legs underneath a non-turning upper body.

BANKING. Banking occurs when you lean toward the inside of a turn with a relatively straight body. This is an inefficient action that requires much upper body movement. Also, it reduces weight on the outside ski of the turn. Sideways slipping or skidding can result. Indications of banking are:

(a) sideways slipping or skidding

(b) tipping the shoulders or head

(c) drop the inside hand

(d) lift the outside hand

(e) too much weight on the inside ski

Lesson Plan:

1. *Upper Body Exercise*, page 77. This exercise uses ski poles, placed around the hips, as a reference to assess and correct unnecessary movement of the upper body.

2. *Angulated Position*, page 113. Angulation is the correct position versus banking.

3. *Wedge/Parallel*, page 114. The angulation acquired in a wedge turn is transferred to a parallel turn.

4. *Arms Crossed*, page 136. Use this exercise to identify inward lean of the upper body and work toward an upright position.

5. *Horizontal Pole*, page 137. This exercise will also help you recognize banking and correct the problem.

EXCESSIVE WEIGHT ON THE INSIDE SKI. Excessive weight on the inside ski decreases the weight on the outside ski. As a result, the outside ski cannot bend sufficiently, or retain the arc that is necessary to carve a turn. The effectiveness of the transition between turns is also diminished when too much weight is on the inside ski. Indications of excessive weight on the inside ski are:

(a) inward lean of the upper body

(b) rotation of the upper body toward the center of the turn

(c) stiff outside leg

(d) fatigue of the inside leg

(e) dropping the inside hand or lifting the outside hand

(f) loss of edge grip with the outside ski

Lesson Plan:

1. Traverse lifting the inside ski repeatedly off the snow.

2. Turn, tapping the inside ski on the snow.

3. *Lift the Inside Ski*, page 97. Lift the inside ski of a turn to improve balance on the outside ski.

4. *One Ski Scooter*, page 58. This exercise is helpful for learning to balance on one ski.

5. *Balance Routine on One Ski*, page 89. Exercises on one ski help to improve your balance.

INSIDE SKI RAISED. Some skiers concentrate their effort so greatly on the outside ski that they lift their inside ski off the snow. In the past, total weight on the outside ski was critical to bend the outside ski and hold it in an arc. Lifting the inside ski to weight the outside ski became the way to ski for many racers. With the soft flex, yet stiff torsional rigidity of skis today, it is not necessary to concentrate weight entirely on one ski. In fact, the benefits of weighting two skis "outweigh" lifting one ski. Indications of lifting the inside ski are:

(a) As weight is transferred to the outside ski, the inside ski is raised off the snow for part of the turn, or the entire turn.

(b) fabric is cut along the inside of your ski pants at boot level

Lesson Plan:

1. Ski with an overly wide stance to develop the concurrent

actions of both feet.

2. *Edge Change*, page 191. Exercises are given to rehearse the tipping movement of both feet and skis.

3. *Link Carved Turns*, page 193. Edge change movements are applied to linked turns.

RAILING. *Railing* occurs when a ski has more edge angle than is necessary ("over-edged"). Generally, railing happens at the start of a turn when the skier moves too far toward the inside of the turn and the edged ski is not weighted sufficiently. The skier expects to ski a sharper radius than the radius the ski actually follows. As a result, the skier has committed too far to the inside of the turn and must recover with the inside ski. Indications of railing are:

(a) the feeling that the ski wants to go straight

(b) falling onto the inside ski at the beginning of the turn

Lesson Plan:

1. *Leg Alignment*, page 254, to assess for cants. ❋

2. *Edge Change*, page 191, to balance on edged skis early in the turn.

3. *Javelin Turns,* page 117, to encourage correct body position and commitment to the outside ski. ❋

APPENDIX II
EQUIPMENT

This appendix covers guidelines for selecting equipment and suiting it to your size and ability. Information is provided about traditional and deep sidecut skis, boots, bindings, under-binding plates, poles, helmets, goggles and leg alignment.

The right equipment and the right fit are essential. Equipment alone cannot make a champion, but it can prevent one from developing. The appropriate equipment is a necessary prerequisite for good technical skiing. You may have experienced, at one time or another, the discomfort and frustration of poorly fitting ski boots, or unsuitable skis. The wrong equipment can encourage the development of bad habits, which are then difficult to break—even on the right equipment. ❄

SKIS

The edges and base of a ski must be tuned and maintained. Dull edges on hard-packed snow, or skis with bases that are higher than the edges (when the ski is held base upward) will cause skis to slide out. When the edges are higher than the bases, the skis will be difficult to turn.

FLEX. It is important for a ski to flex sufficiently in order to bend an edged ski into an arc to make a turn. If a ski is too stiff, it will not stay in the arc; sideways skidding will occur. Flex, and other ski characteristics such as sidecut, length and torsional rigidity, are covered in *Ski Design*, Chapter 1, *A Curved Path*.

SIZE. Selection of the best length and model of skis depends on your size, ability level and desired performance. A longer ski is more stable at high speed while a shorter ski is more manageable and easier to turn. Follow these general guidelines to check for appropriate ski length on traditional skis.

  (a) Beginning skiers: shoulder height skis are easy to maneuver.

  (b) Intermediate skiers: skis that reach somewhere between the nose and the top of the head. Skiers at this level can handle a little longer ski that is still easy to maneuver.

(c) Advanced skiers: skis that are as tall as their height and up to a height of the width of their hand above their head. This length allows skiers to be stable at higher speeds.

(d) Technically strong skiers who ski three or more days per week: longer skis which range from a height of their hand's width above the head up to the height of the wrist when their arm is extended. At this level, skiers should have the technical skills that are necessary to ski on longer skis.

As a general rule, skiers on deep sidecut skis can ski a length that is ten centimeters shorter than their recommended length on traditional skis. ❄

DEEP SIDECUT SKIS

The information that follows is specific to deep sidecut skis. There are many terms to identify deep sidecut skis. Some of the names include, super sidecut, maxcut, shaped skis, parabolic and hourglass.

SIDECUT RADIUS. Deep sidecut skis fall into two general categories determined by *sidecut radius*. Sidecut radius refers to the measurement of the tightest radius a ski of a particularly length will carve a turn. One category includes skis that turn in a distance of less than 20 meters. The other group consists of skis that carve a turn within 20–30 meters. As a reference, the radius of traditional skis measures 35—50 meters. Also, keep in mind that the length of the ski affects the sidecut radius. A short ski will turn in a tighter arc than a longer ski, assuming that the tip, waist and tail dimensions are the same.

The shorter radius skis tend to have deeper than usual sidecuts. They are designed specifically for carving. Since the tip and tail of these skis are so flared, they tend not to pivot or skid well. These skis provide a tool for skiers to improve their carving skill. Also, they carve tight, round turns at relatively slow speeds effectively.

Deep sidecut skis that have a sidecut radius of 20–30 meters are more versatile in terms of speed and terrain. These skis are skied at traditional lengths or more typically, ten centimeters shorter. Although some designs are more radical than others, the more versatile sidecuts can slip and skid as well as carve and are, therefore, superb all-mountain skis.

WIDTH AT WAIST. Another measurement that is used to differentiate between skis is the width at the waist. Although this does not reflect the difference in tip, waist and tail dimensions, it is a useful measurement in conjunction with the sidecut radius dimension. Some skis tend to be wider underfoot for stability, yet they sport the same sidecut as narrower skis.

SOFT FLEX. Deep sidecut skis tend to be softer flexing than their traditional counterparts. Skis that have a soft longitudinal flex (along the length) are easier to turn, flex deeply to maximize the carving effect of a given sidecut, and handle bumps and terrain changes smoothly. Years ago, it was difficult for ski manufacturers to produce soft flexing skis and still maintain adequate torsional strength. Previous attempts at soft skis failed because the tips and tails would twist off the torsional axis and cause skidding to occur. Modern construction techniques allow longitudinal and torsional flex to be isolated so that a ski can be longitudinally soft while maintaining torsional strength.

A soft flexing ski allows a skier to distribute more weight to the inside ski. Any time weight is distributed between two skis (instead of one), less pressure is applied to each ski. With a soft flexing ski, less pressure is necessary to bend the ski into an arc. However, it still can support the pressure applied if the skier only weights the outside ski in the turn.

STABILITY. Skiers that have the ability to carve turns find deep sidecut skis very stable. Once an arc is obtained, the skis tend to stay on edge and continue the arc ("locked on edge"). For skiers that have not learned to carve, or carve only a portion of a turn, deep sidecut skis may seem unsteady. This is a function of the width of the tip or tail "catching" in the snow during a skidded phase of a turn.

BENEFITS FOR BEGINNERS. Deep sidecut skis can greatly benefit beginning skiers. It is often helpful to start on a soft flexing, shorter length ski, such as a 150 centimeter sidecut ski. Beginners can move to carving very quickly on deep sidecut skis.

BENEFITS FOR INTERMEDIATES. Intermediate skiers have basic skills in place and can benefit greatly from deep sidecut skis. The primary advantage is better performance with less work. For the intermediate, carving will be a new sensation that will provide control—something that is continually strived for in skiing.

BENEFITS FOR EXPERTS. Expert skiers know how to ski, but consistency can be elusive. Deep sidecut skis make it easier to perform optimal turns more frequently. They require less effort and are, therefore, more fun. An incredible sensation caused by G Forces occurs when you "load" (bend skis into a deep arc) these skis in a tightly carved turn. Any skier who can carve turns will find a heightened carving experience on deep sidecut skis.

Some skiing techniques do not lend well to deep sidecut skis. If you would rather keep your skis under your body, you may prefer a traditional ski. Characteristics of this skiing style include, a narrower stance and a controlled skid to an edge set.

BENEFITS FOR RACERS. There has been a significant trend toward deep sidecuts in racing for a number of years. Very recently, however, non-racing skis have surpassed racing skis in terms of depth of sidecut.

"The degree to which racing skis will follow is a bit unclear, although I think racing skis will gradually move in this direction. Young racers who are still developing skills and have less strength will definately race on the new deep sidecut skis. They will achieve greater performance more quickly on these new skis, and they will continue to use new technology as they rise to the highest levels of the sport. This situation is comparable to the oversize racquets in tennis where the top competitors

were the last to change to the new technology."
—Charlie Adams, Director of Product Development,
Dynastar Skis

Deep sidecut skis are very applicable to Giant Slalom. Younger racers will begin using deep sidecuts in Giant Slalom immediately, and as they mature, these skis will most likely become the standard.

The application for Super G is much the same as for Giant Slalom. The deep sidecut skis will be more important for the turnier, more Giant Slalom style courses.

Modern Downhill skis have enormous sidecuts compared to their predecessors. They may be influenced by the developments in Giant Slalom, but not to the same extent.

The application of deep sidecut skis to Slalom has occurred more slowly. Only recently, have increased sidecut designs become accepted in Slalom.

EDGE BEVEL. The side and bottom of the ski's metal edge is beveled to create a sharper edge angle than ninety degrees. *Bevel* refers to the angle at which the metal slants. Typically, a deep side-cut ski will be tuned with one half (1/2) of a degree of bevel on the base of the ski. Two degrees of bevel on the side of the edge is recommended for a recreational skier. Three degrees of side bevel is recommended for a racer. The tips and tails should be beveled in the same way, and not rounded. The amount of bevel at the tip (above the turning surface) can be increased. ❄

BOOTS

S **TANCE.** Ski boots should permit a balanced, natural stance. In most instances, a boot should be soft enough (flex forward without great force) to flex comfortably. A soft boot that will "give" allows you to use subtle movements to control your skis. The sense of balance learned in a soft boot will help you develop a light touch on your skis and a "feel" for the snow. If your boots are too stiff, ski shop personnel may be able to modify them so that they can be flexed more easily.

Choose a four buckle, front-entry boot rather than a rear-entry boot. Four buckle boots can give a more personal fit and place you in a better balanced position. Rear-entry boots may not provide enough support when you lean against the back of the boot. When flexed, they usually do not "give" but spring back instead. This can cause your weight to move back toward your heels. Then, too, with a looser fit, the foot tends to slide forward in the boot, shifting weight back.

SIZE. Your boot should fit snugly around your foot and leg for control. To determine if your boots fit properly, follow these steps:

(a) Remove the liner from the shell.

(b) Step into the shell, and while standing, slide your foot forward so that your toes just touch the end of the shell. There should be a 1/4–1/2 inch gap between the heel and the back of the shell to allow for the liner.

(c) Put on the liner while wearing one pair of warm socks. There should be enough room so that your toes do not press into the end of the liner.

(d) With the liner in the shell, adjust the buckles so that the boots fit snugly. Flex forward as you buckle each boot in order to push the heel into the back of the liner.

(e) Do your feet hurt anywhere? Try to identify the exact location of any sore spots. Then take off the boots and socks and look for any red marks which may indicate pressure points. Ski shop personnel can often correct any problems.

Walk around in the boots and go up and down stairs, holding the railing. You should be able to walk reasonably well. If you are very clumsy and unbalanced, the boots may be too stiff, too tall, too large, or a combination of these. In a boot that is too large, the foot can move excessively and be unstable while skiing. A boot that is too small can cause pain, numbness and cold feet.

To minimize wear from walking, it is helpful to use boot sole protectors, plastic guards that attach to the bottom of ski boots.

FLEX. To determine if you can flex a boot sufficiently, move down and up, from a tall stance by bending the ankle. Beginning skiers can practice this action first without boots to attain the correct body position. Try not to sit back or bend forward in an effort to flex the boot. Either of these movements indicate that the boot is too stiff. Another test is to try to jump since jumping is very difficult when boots are too stiff.

CARVING BOOTS. Ski boot design is changing to coincide with deep sidecut skis. Features include greater lateral strength to support extreme lateral movements and softer forward flex to allow for subtle fore/aft movements. Some boots have a narrower sole and are less bulky above the inside edge to help prevent the boot from touching the snow when the ski is tipped on an extreme edge angle. ✳

BINDINGS

Binding manufacturers recommend that the complete ski/binding/boot system be inspected by an authorized retailer before each ski season. Also, have bindings checked during the season to ensure appropriate settings as you become a better skier. Do not increase the settings if you release out of your bindings with no apparent cause. Instead, have the ski/binding/boot system checked by an authorized retailer for re-adjustment.

"DIN" setting charts are used to determine binding settings. The DIN number represents the amount of energy that it takes to release from the binding. Factors that are used to determine a skier's DIN setting are age, weight, boot sole length and skiing ability. The binding will function better if the setting is not right at the low or high end of the DIN range.

Be sure to clear all of the dirt, snow or ice off your boots before stepping into your bindings (FIGURE II.1). It is all too easy to overlook this, particularly when you are skiing with a group that is in a hurry to get going. ✳

UNDER-BINDING PLATES

Under-binding plates are known as lifters, risers, platforms and spacers. When deep sidecut or race skis are bowed into a deep arc and edge angle is extreme, the inside of the boot on the outside ski can contact the snow ("boot out") and tumble the skier. Therefore, lifts are added under the bindings to raise the skier and avoid boot-out. The added height of an under-binding plate allows greater leverage capability. Therefore, less fore/aft body movement is necessary to increase pressure on the tip or tail of the ski. Some plates feature shock-dampening qualities that help to stabilize shorter-length deep sidecut skis at high speeds.

Some ski bindings incorporate a plate that can be adjusted at the skier's descretion to make the ski stiffer. This is helpful for changes in speed, terrain or snow conditions. The adjustable plate is especially beneficial on the softer flexing all-mountain deep sidecut skis. The soft flex that allows the ski to bend deeply with slight pressure can be stiffened to meet the demands of speed on an icy course. In this way, it is like having more than one pair of skis. ❄

POLES

POLE LENGTH. To check for the proper pole length, stand in your ski boots on a flat surface. Turn your pole over so that the tip is facing up. Grasp the pole right below the basket. Your forearm should be parallel to the ground with your elbow touching your side (FIGURE II.2). If your hand is higher than your elbow, the poles can be cut down to the correct size at a ski shop.

POLE GRIP. Pole grips with straps are recommended. Plastic strapless grips leave the thumbs more susceptible to injuries and do not allow for a proper pole swing. Select straps that are easy to put on, adjust, and hold adjustment. To use properly, your hand goes up through the loop of the strap, and then down, gripping the strap and the pole. Fit each strap so that it is snug around your glove when your hand is positioned at the top of the grip. ❄

GOGGLES

Goggles provide the best eye protection. Sunglasses are more apt to break and they allow potentially damaging rays and wind to enter through the sides of the glasses.

Goggles should have appropriate lenses. On sunny or hazy days use dark lenses for adequate sun protection. On dark, snowy days, use lighter lenses for better visibility. Look for goggles with interchangeable lenses to avoid buying two pairs. It is important to take care of the goggle lenses so that they stay clean and free of scratches. ❄

HELMETS

FIGURE II.3

Helmets are made to fit comfortably and be protective.

Ski helmets are recommended for all-day wear. Helmet technology has evolved tremendously in recent years. Its development coincides, in a timely manner, with growth in the ski industry. Groomed slopes and high performance equipment allow skiers to reach high speeds. Obstacles such as signs, trees, snow-making machinery, and lift towers are present. Ski slopes are often crowded, with skiers of different ages, skill levels, and speed capability sharing the same terrain. Considering these factors, it makes good sense to use a helmet (FIGURE II.3).

"In the very near future, helmets will become the norm because they simply are better and more beneficial than any other headgear. The trend has begun as more and more alpine enthusiasts wear helmets every year. The technology of the 1990's offers the materials and design capabilities to produce a variety of helmet models that meet the specific needs of skiers and snowboarders. The development process is not stagnant. More futuristic designs, with improved features such as better impact management, venting, and integrated eye wear will become available soon." (FIGURE II.4) —Marc P. Hauser, President, MPH Associates, Inc.

FEATURES. Necessary features for all-day wear, Slalom, or Giant Slalom helmets include:

(a) a hard plastic shell that is shatter and puncture resistant, providing protection against sharp objects such as ski edges and immovable objects such as rocks and trees.

(b) an expanded polystyrene liner that partially absorbs the

shock of an impact

(c) padding for a personalized, snug fit and for warmth
(d) an open ear design that does not disturb hearing or balance
(e) an under-the-chin strap that positions the helmet properly and secures the fit

Optional features include:

(a) a padded rim for extra protection of the face
(b) jaw protection with a removable piece for added protection of the face and teeth
(c) bright colors and graphics for high visibility.

FIGURE II.4 (top)
Helmet technology is rapidly developing.

FIT AND SIZE. When it comes to selecting a helmet, correct fit is crucial. To ensure a secure fit, ski helmets should be worn without a hat underneath. The liner of the helmet provides the warmth of a hat. A helmet that is too large will not be as effective in preventing injury because the head can hit the inside of the helmet upon impact. In addition, a helmet that is too large can be too heavy.

Correct helmet size can be determined by measuring the head circumference (in inches or centimeters) and then referring to the manufacturer's sizing chart. Padding can be adjusted or added to ensure a snug and comfortable fit. When an incorrectly sized helmet is excessively padded, protection is compromised, just as excessive padding in too large a ski boot hinders performance. Helmet manufacturers offer sizes ranging from very small helmets for children (FIGURE II.5) to extra-large helmets for adults. Various models are designed to meet the needs of all-day wear and the different demands of racing. It is important to use the appropriate model for the situation.

Many people are unaware of the protective values of ski helmets. In other sports that involve speed, obstacles, collisions, and possible contact with stationary objects, protective head gear has evolved to be an accepted part of the athlete's equipment. Football, hockey, bicycling and in-line skating are examples (FIGURE II.6). ❉

FIGURE II.5
Children's moves can be unpredictable, and it is common for them to dart across a busy slope, perhaps to ski into the woods in search of adventure on a "tree trail." They need the protection of a helmet.

FIGURE II.6
Helmets provide a valuable level of added protection from the dangers of high speed collisions.

LEG ALIGNMENT

I n a hip-angulated position, the upper body stays relatively vertical while the lower body is at a slant to the snow. This is a strong position because it aligns the foot with the knee and the hip in a relatively straight line for support. When the skier's bone structure is aligned, the forces that act on the skis are transmitted through the body in the most efficient manner. As a result, there is less stress on the joints, muscular effort is minimized, and better body position can be achieved. To attain optimum positioning, a skier may need better foot support, angling of the cuff of the boot, or adjustments in the angle at which the boot makes contact with the ski.

In a static position, the ideal alignment of the body in relation to the ski occurs when the ski is flat and the center of the knee mass is slightly to the inside of a line between the hips and the center of the ski boot. Consider a skier who is aligned with the knee to the outside of the center line of the boot on a flat ski. This position is typical of a bow-legged skier. As the skier moves the knee over the center of the boot, edging will occur. When the foot and hip are aligned in the turn, the skier will have more edge angle than is necessary; too much edge. To achieve less edge angle, the skier has to reduce the amount of knee, and/or hip angulation, sacrificing foot to hip alignment. In this circumstance, the outside knee often wobbles in and out as the skier wavers between too much edge angle and too much knee angulation. To improve alignment, add the thick side of a cant (wedge) to the outside edge of the ski (FIGURE II.7). This helps to re-position the skier's knee to the inside of the center mark of the boot when the ski is flat. After re-alignment, the skier can use knee angulation without over-edging the ski.

In the case of a knock-kneed skier who is aligned with the knee too far to the inside of the center line of the boot, the thick side of the cant should be added to the inside edge of the ski. This will bring the knee in a position that is about one centimeter to the inside of the center line of the boot. When the knee is too far inside, the ski remains flat while knee and/or hip angles already occur. This skier has to move extremely to the inside of the turn or tuck one knee behind the other in order to get enough edge to grip the snow. In this circumstance, the outside ski often rails; continues on a straight course without turning. When the skier's alignment is corrected with canting, the skier can use knee angulation

FIGURE II.7

Cants can be added under the binding to improve leg alignment over the ski.

and achieve sufficient edge angle.

Body/ski alignment can be affected by the position of the foot in the boot. An unsupported or fatigued foot can alter knee alignment. The upper cuff of the boot can negatively affect alignment when it does not correspond with the curvature of the lower leg. Individual body characteristics, such as different leg lengths and femoral rotation, also effect alignment.

Improved structural alignment can be attained through a three step process:

(1) Support the foot with an orthotic device or molded foot-bed.
(2) Adjust the angle of the upper cuff to correspond with the angle of the lower leg.
(3) Cant, if necessary, to achieve optimum knee alignment between the boot and the hip.

FOOT SUPPORT. Leg alignment will be different for a non-supported foot (the arch flattens and the foot can tip inward) compared to a supported foot. When the foot is supported, it stays in a strong position and does not flatten when the boot is buckled. It is also important for the boot to be the correct size in order to provide good support. An arch support, custom-molded foot-bed, or orthotic device can be added to, or replace the insole, depending on the amount of support that is best for each person. Besides helping to align the body effectively, personalized insoles can make your boots more comfortable. Boot fitting specialists at retail stores can help to assess your needs.

UPPER CUFF ADJUSTMENT. After the foot is sufficiently supported, adjust the upper cuff of the boot so that the lower leg is centered in the cuff. To find the centered position, remove the liner, place the foot-bed in the boot shell and adjust the cuff allowing equal space on either side of the leg. After this adjustment is made, the angle of the boot cuff will not force the lower leg into an unnatural position. Since not all boots have cant adjustments, skiers that have significant lower leg curvature should select a boot that does adjust. If this is not possible, have the adjustment made by canting under the binding.

CANTS. The angle at which the boot makes contact with the ski is altered with the use of wedges, or *cants*. Typically, this is accomplished by placing cants under the bindings. Some racers have the soles of their boots planed or sanded to achieve the appropriate angle. Material is then added to the top of the toe and heel to return the thickness to DIN specifications. This is an expensive process and it is not always an available option. Some skiers choose to have their boot soles altered rather than canting many pairs of skis. This also allows them to switch their right and left skis in order to have "new" inside edges for racing.

Follow these steps to determine if, and to what extent, cants are necessary. You will need another person to help you.

(a) Stand in your boots (buckled for skiing) and skis on a flat floor.

(b) Place your skis in a parallel position. Your skis should be about hip width apart. Stand in a balanced position with your joints flexed and your eyes looking ahead.

(c) Flatten your skis against the floor.

(d) Have another person mark a line on your knee cap to indicate the center of your knee mass.

(e) Have the helper hang a plumb bob (string with a pointed weight) from this mark and draw a line on the boot toe where the plumb bob points.

(f) Use strips of duct tape under the inside or outside edge of the ski to position the point of the plumb bob one centimeter to the inside (toward the big toe) of the center line on the boot.

(g) Measure the thickness of the duct tape to determine how thick the cant should be.

(h) Have a qualified boot fitter (an alignment specialist) at a retail store add cants under your bindings. The Lange ski boot company has developed a device that is available in many ski shops for the purpose of making alignment assessments. ❄

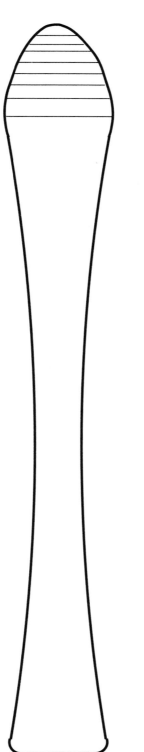

APPENDIX III
SKI PATTERN

Use this pattern in conjunction with the exercise, *Model the Ski* in Chapter 1, *A Curved Path*. Copy this page, glue it onto thin cardboard and cut the cardboard to match the shape of the ski. ❄

LESSON PLAN WORKSHEET

You may copy this worksheet to use with the *Lesson Plan* information provided in Chapters 2–8.

WARM YOUR BODY.
Warm-up Exercises:
Stretching Exercises:

RHYTHM and REVIEW.
Topics to keep in mind:

DIRECTED FREE SKIING.
Names of slopes:
Focus:

SCHOOLWORK.
Name of "practice hill:"
Specific exercises:

MOUNTAIN PLAYGROUND.
Names of slopes:

SLOW and EASY.
Name of slope:
Focus:

Skiing and the *Art* of Carving

In the following, bold face numbers refer to page numbers for photographs or illustrations.

INDEX

Angulation
   hip, 113, **113**, **114**, 187, **187**
   knee, 113, **114**
Arc
   foot, 101 **101**
   round arc, 195, **197**
   segment of turn, 48, **49**
   study, 80
Arms crossed, 136, **136**
Auditory perception, 226

Balance point
   deep sidecut, 54, **54**, 185, 186
   traditional, 53, **53**
Balance routine
   one ski, 89, **89**
   two skis, 60, **60**
Balanced stance, 52, **52**, 53, **53**, 113
Banking, 115, **115**
Bend and extend turns, 201, **201**, 202, **202**
Bevel, 248
Bobbing, 98, **99**
Boot turns, 94, **94**
Bump skiing
   jump in, 157, **157**
   line, 155, **156**, 157, 158
   small bumps, 82, 103, **103**
   technique, 104, 126, **126**, 155, **155**
   wedge, 82, **82**

Cants, 254–256, **254**
Carving
   deep sidecut, 184, **184**, 185, 193, **194**
   description, 31, 44, 47
   direct carve progression, 189–206
   model, 48, **50**
   parallel, 102, **102**
   wedge, 75, **75**
Centrifugal, 187, 199
Charleston, 142, **142**
Correcting Errors, 235–243
Countered position

traverse, 116
turn, 116, **116**
Crayon mark, 97
Cross-over transition, 121, **121**
Cross-under transition, 121, **121**

Deep sidecut skis
    description, 31, 49
    equipment information, 245–248
    notes for, 54, 70, 77, 113, 120, 122, 130
Deep sidecut carve, 183–210, **184, 187–198, 200–202, 204–206**
Diagonal descent, **195, 196**
Direct carve progression, 189–207
Directed free skiing, 30, 37, 66, 84, 107, 126, 158, 180, 208
Dynamic carved turns
    deep sidecut skis, 199–201, **200**
    traditional skis, 110, **110**
Dynamic skiing, 109–128

Edge bevel, 248
Edge change, 191–194, **192, 193**
Edging
    deep sidecut, 188
    mechanics of, 47, **47**
Edge locks, **76**, 77
Equipment 244–254
    bindings, 250, **250**
    boots, 248–250
    cants, 254–256, **254**
    goggles, 252
    helmets, 252–253, **252, 253**
    poles, 251, **251**
    skis, 244–248
    under-binding plates, 251

Floaters, 119, **119**, 120
Flow, 120, **120**
Formation skiing, 143–146
    synchronized turns, 143, **143**
    opposite turns, 144, **144**
    lead-follow, 145, **145**
    synchronized speed play, 145, **145**
    synchronized circle, 146, **146**
    line pull-out, 146
    long and short medley, 146, **147**

Garland turns, 96–97, **96**
    converging step, 172–173, **174**
    parallel step, 165, **167**
Getting up, 55, **55**, 56, **56**

Hand turns, 80, **81**
Hold hands, 137, **138**
Hop Turns 138–142
    one foot, 139, **139**
    outside foot, 140, **141**
    turn entry, 140, **140**
    turn entry, outside ski, 142, **142**
    two foot, 139, **139**
    without skis, 138, **138**, 140, **140**
Horizontal pole, 137, **137**

Inside ski, 45, **45**, 74, 88, **88**
    lead, 188, **188**
    lift ski, 97, **97**
    steer, 179

Javelin, 117, **117**, 118,**118**

Lead-follow, 81, **81**
Leaping, 97, **98**
Leg alignment, 254–256
Lesson Planning
    description, 32, 36–38
    within chapters, 65–66, 84–86, 106–108, 126–128, 158–160, 180–182, 207–209
    Lesson Plan Example, 67, 85, 108, 127, 128, 159, 160, 182, 209, 210
Lesson Plan Worksheet, 258

Mountain playground, 31, 38, 67, 85, 108, 127, 159, 181, 208
    narrative, 227

One ski
    lift ski, 111, **111**
    remove ski, 112
    one pole, 132, **133**
    no poles, 134, **134**
One ski scooter, 58, **59**
Outside ski, 45, **45**, 72

Parallel turns, 87–108, 88, **88**
Perceptual skills, 222–226
Pole action
    across flats 78, **79**
    description, 78, 100, **100**, **101**, 155, **155**
    double pole plant, 150, **151**
    incorrect action, 100, 122, 238
    strap, 78, **78**
    swing, 100, **100**, 148, **148**
    without, 130, **132**, 134
Pivoting, 49
Pivot slip, 94, **94**
Pull feet back, 203, 204, **204**

Quick turns, 129–160
    description, 130, **131**

Radius
    long, 80, 102, 120
    short, 80, 102, 130, 152, 204, 205, **205**
Rebound, 106, 142
Reverse 180 turn, 206, **206**
Retraction turn, 202, 203
Royal, 112, **112**
Rhythm and review, 37, 66, 84, 106, 126, 158, 180, 207, 208

Safety stop, 95, **95**
Schoolwork, 38, 66, 85, 107, 126, 158, 180, 181, 208
Sidecut radius, 245
Sideslip, 92, **93**
    forward sideslip, **93**, 94
Sidestep, 57
    in traverse, 164, **165**, 165, **166**
    over objects, 58, **58**
    over poles, 61, 90, **90**, 164, **164**
    shadow chase, 91, **91**
Skating, 99, **99**, 178, **178**, **179**
Skidding, 49, 102, **102**
Ski design
    flex, 46, **46**, **47**
    length, 46
    sidecut, 45, **45**, 245–248
    torsional rigidity, 46, **46**
Ski pattern, **257**
Sliding, 49, 56, **56**, 60

Slipping, 49
Slow and Easy, 38, 67, 85, 108, 127, 159, 182, 209
Snow conditions
    crud, 84, 155
    hard snow and ice, 83, 105
    deep snow and powder, 83, 106, **106**, 154, **154**
Speed
    control of, 80, 102
    chart, 120
    increase, 197, **197**
    adjusting, 224, 225
Steering, 49
Stem, 170
Step turns 161–182
    converging step, 169–174
    diverging step, 175–180
    parallel step, 162–168
Stretching exercises, 215–217, **215–219**
Surveyor's tape, 148, **149**

Tactile and visual perception, 224–226, **225**, **226**
Target skiing, 134, **134**
    moving target, 134, **135**
Terrain
    bumps (see bump skiing)
    gentle, 82, 102, 124
    steep terrain, 82, 124
    terrain features/garden, 104, 105
    variable, 82, **83**
Traverse
    deep sidecut, 189, **189**, 190, **190**, 191, **191**
    exercises, 91, 92, **92**, 116, **116**
    position, 91, **91**
Tuck turns, 136, **136**
Turn shape
    "C," 122, **123**
    "comma," 123, **123**
    deep sidecut, 188, **188**
    "J," 123, **123**
    smooth transition between, 152
    vary, 123, 151, 152, 168
Two skis, 187, **187**

Upper Body
    direction of, 118, **118**

movement of, 135, **135**
wedge, 72, **73**, 77, **78**

Verbal cue, 73, 148, **150**
Visual perception, 222–226, **222**, **223**

Wagon wheel, 171, **171**, 177, **177**
Walking, 55, **55**, 57, **58**
Warm-up exercises, 212–215, **212–215**
Warm your body, 36, 65
Wedge
    position, 61, **62**
    sliding, 62, **63**
    stopping, 63, **64**
    turning, 69–86, **71**
    wedge/parallel, 64, **64**, **65**, 72, **72**, 114, **114**
    width, 63, **63**, 77, **77**
Wide stance, 186, **186**
Zig-zag drill, 171, **171**

For her writings, Ellen Post Foster has drawn from her extensive background as both a junior and an international competitor. Her skiing career began in 1968 as a member of the Jiminy Peak Junior Demonstration Team in Massachusetts. The program emphasized perfecting fundamental skills which proved to provide a strong technical base and theme for her later accomplishments. The demonstration team evolved into a junior freestyle team, preparing Ellen to become a world-class competitor on the professional freestyle tour in 1974. Ellen placed second overall in the 1975 Freestyle World Championships and is the only person to ever win an international aerial, ballet, mogul and combined event all in the same year. Interestingly, Alan Schönberger coached her in ballet, leading to this achievement. Never losing sight of the impact of her junior team experiences, Ellen directed her education to teaching and coaching. She was a member of the Professional Ski Instructors of America National Demonstration Team from 1980 to 1988. This privilege is shared by ten of the most talented technical skiers/ski educators in the nation who are selected every four years. Ellen was also a member of two U. S. *Interski* teams that performed in Italy and Canada. *Interski* is the international forum for the sharing of skiing and teaching methods between skiing nations world-wide. Ellen is the author of four technical books on skiing and ski racing. She received the Russell Wilder Memorial Award from US Skiing in recognition of her "outstanding achievements in focusing the interests of America's youth on the sport of skiing." ❄

Alan Schönberger is a world champion skier and performance artist as well as a photographer. His pictorial studies of skiing are founded on an extensive background as a ski educator and an international competitor.

Alan studied photography at Utah State University and taught skiing at Alta and Snowbird during the wintertime. Summers were spent in New York City where he continued studies as a student of Robert Joffrey Ballet and Merce Cunningham Dance. He also studied with mime great, Moni Yakim, who recognized Alan's passion for physical comedy, dance and skiing. He urged a movement piece on skis. Alan pursued the unusual outdoor stage venue that

Opening ceremonies,
1994 World Cup in Vail

the competitive sport of freestyle ballet skiing provided. His variety of dance, clown and skiing forms interfused at an international freestyle skiing competition which he won. For the next three years, Alan dominated freestyle events in Europe, Canada and the U. S., and earned the World Trophy in Ski Ballet in 1976.

The need to bring his work into a more formal theatrical environment ultimately prevailed. He created the theatrical touring production, *Piano Roll,* with the help of Ellen Post Foster. Alan set out to ski the great stages in theatres across the country on the music roll of a larger than life player piano. His extensive and varied performances have toured thirty-three states and four foreign countries including a performance live with the Rochester Philharmonic Orchestra and a PBS feature. He returned to the snow in 1994 to perform in the opening ceremony for the World Cup in Vail, Colorado. ✶

THE TURNING POINT SKI FOUNDATION

The first time Ellen Post Foster and Alan Schönberger met and began working together was in 1974 while they were competing on the International Freestyle circuit. In 1992, they founded the Turning Point Ski Foundation, a non-profit organization to help young skiers strive for excellence. Through skiing, children can experience the joy of movement, the thrill of meeting challenges and the inexpressible wonder of success.

In the past four years, Foster and Schönberger have authored, photographed and published numerous articles and four books to help better educate the parents, instructors and coaches of children. All of the proceeds from these books and from *Skiing and the Art of Carving* fund the foundation to be used for future educational projects. ✶

Jay Evans

Steve Olwin

Tony Russo

ABOUT THE DEMONSTRATORS

Jay Evans is in his third term and ninth year on the P.S.I.A. National Demonstration Team. He has represented the U. S. at *Interski* in Austria and Japan. This is Jay's sixteenth year at the Vail/Beaver Creek Ski School. He has been a training supervisor for eleven years and he currently works on special projects and staff training. Jay is a P.S.I.A. Certification Examiner and a U. S. Ski Coaches Association Level III coach. Jay lives in Minturn, Colorado.

Steve Olwin is a member of the P.S.I.A.-North West Technical Team. He is a P.S.I.A. Examiner and a U. S. Ski Coaches Association Level III coach. Steve has coached for Stevens Pass Alpine Club for nine years and he was a P.S.I.A. National Children's Committee member for six years. Steve lives in Seattle, Washington where he is an aeronautical engineer.

Tony Russo is the Program Director for Gymnastics in the Vail Recreation District. He is a former gymnast at Arizona State University and has coached gymnastics for fifteen years. He lives at the foot of Vail mountain. ❄

The printing of this book was made possible through generous contributions from *Dynastar* skis, *Lange* boots, *Kerma* poles, *MPH Associates, Inc.* (distributor of *Boeri* helmets), *Marker* bindings, *Bolle* goggles, *Arapahoe Basin Resort*, and the *Turning Point Ski Foundation*. In addition, grants were provided by the *PSIA–Northwest* division's *Education Foundation* and *PSIA–Rocky Mountain* division's *Education Foundation*. Clothing was provided by *Schure Sports U.S.A. Inc.* (distributor of *Phenix* skiwear).

T he "demonstration team" for *Skiing and the Art of Carving* used equipment from the following companies. To learn more about their products, information can be obtained by contacting the companies directly.

EQUIPMENT INFORMATION

Dynastar, Lange, Kerma
P.O. Box 25, Hercules Drive
Colchester, VT 05446-0025
Phone: 802.655.2400 Fax: 802.655.4329
www.dynastar.com

Boeri Sport USA
MPH Associates, Inc.
PO Box 567
Norwood, MA 02062
Phone: 617.551.9933
www.boeri.com/mph

Marker USA
PO Box 26548
Salt Lake City, UT 84126
Phone: 801.972.2100 Fax: 801.973.7241

Bolle America, Inc.
3890 Elm Street
Denver, CO 80207
Phone: 303.321.4300 Fax: 303.321.6952

Phenix
Schure Sports U.S.A. Inc.
161 Deerhide Crescent, Unit 9A
Weston, Ontario
M9M 2Z2
Canada
Phone: 416.741.2119 Fax: 416.741.2388

Moriarty Hat & Sweater Co.
112 Main Street, Box 1117
Stowe, VT 05672
Phone: 802.253.4052

ORDERING INFORMATION

To order additional copies of *Skiing and the Art of Carving,* and any of the following books or video, please send your name, address, and cost of book(s) plus $4.95 shipping and handling to:

Turning Point Ski Foundation
PO Box 943
Edwards, CO 81632

Free Carve Skiing
$29.95
(Video)

Free Carve Skiing is all about developing and refining the skills to unlock the power of contemporary equipment. Based on the book *Skiing and the Art of Carving,* the video reveals the way in which advanced ski design can contribute to friendly, realistic accomplishments. It demonstrates how a carving ski, when properly tipped on edge and balanced upon, turns naturally, eliminating the need for difficult-to-learn movements. *Free Carve Skiing* features exclusive footage of Olympic gold medalist, Tommy Moe, and National Demonstration Team members, Jay Evans and Ellen Post Foster. Filmed by cinematographer and World Champion skier, Alan Schönberger, *Free Carve Skiing* is a compelling visual study of state of the art skiing.

Technical Skills for Alpine Skiing
$15.95
(Book)

Technical Skills for Alpine Skiing contains numerous exercises that teach and refine skiing skills in a very progressive manner beginning with wedge turns and building to expert skiing. Hundreds of photographs of talented young demonstrators enhance a clear and descriptive text. True narratives precede each chapter.

Race Skills for Alpine Skiing
$14.95
(Book)

Race Skills for Alpine Skiing is an instructional book that teaches skiers to become racers and racers to become champions. It provides a wealth of information for aspiring racers as well as experienced competitors. Distinct chapters cover Giant Slalom, Slalom, and the speed events of Super-G and Downhill. Preface by Tommy Moe, 1994 Olympic gold and silver medalist.

Conditioning Skills for Alpine Skiing
$11.95
(Book)

Conditioning Skills for Alpine Skiing is an instructional book for parents, coaches and athletes about training for skiing. Only this book provides a conditioning program for children that is specific to the movement patterns found in skiing. Weekly and daily workouts are explained and examples are given. Each workout is comprised of a warm-up session, specific exercises and games to develop skills, a cross-training activity, and a cool-down. Unique to this book are on-the-snow conditioning exercises—on skis. ❄

Visit our web site at: www.tpsf.org
E-mail: skibooks@tpsf.org

Michael Nyman

Much has changed since I began to ski. At that time, wooden skis, cable bindings and clip-on safety straps were the norm. My leather boots were oversized and laced tight with a skating hook.

I remember my transition to leather-plastic laminate, buckle boots and shiny fiberglass skis. I was very excited, and then disappointed. My state-of-the art equipment did not perform the same as my treasured old leather boots and wooden skis. I found it difficult to let go of familiar sensations. Yet before long, I was consumed with the inexpressible joy of learning something new, the desire to do something better, and the excitement of doing it over and over again. Perhaps equipment will always change, but the emotions are timeless.

Ellen Post Foster